FRANKLIN D. ROOSEVELT
AND THE SUPREME COURT

Problems in American Civilization

UNDER THE EDITORIAL DIRECTION OF *George Rogers Taylor*

FRANKLIN D. ROOSEVELT
AND THE SUPREME COURT

EDITED WITH AN INTRODUCTION BY

Alfred Haines Cope
Fred Krinsky

Maxwell School of Citizenship and Public Affairs
Syracuse University

Problems in American Civilization

D. C. HEATH AND COMPANY: Boston

INTRODUCTION

THE Supreme Court of the United States has been a symbol of final and even-handed justice to some, an example of class interest to others, and to still others simply a necessary device for getting a final, if not always prompt, decision upon close legal arguments. Opponents of the Court have said that it converted clauses designed to protect individual freedom into legal ramparts for the defense of entrenched wealth. Proponents have, with steady fingers, pointed to the so-called conservative Court, and reminded its critics of numerous decisions which have maintained essential civil liberties.

It has been popular on the part of some to praise John Marshall, or Louis Brandeis, but to roll their eyes in smug scorn or query at the dictums of Taney, Chase, Miller, Field, or the recent, legally conservative, and persistent Justice Sutherland. Rather than develop stereotyped thinking or judge on a popular basis it is well to re-examine the burning legal issue of the 1930's, to take the modern instance when the usually quiet and unobtrusive candle of the law met a reforming administration and fired a raging public controversy. It was this dispute over Court packing which may well have decided the future of the Supreme Court for decades to come. It is in this dispute that persons may find an opportunity to re-examine the relationship of executives, legislatures, and courts.

To the person who desires to acquaint himself or renew acquaintanceship with the Supreme Court packing controversy and its ramifications, the general problem is simply: *Should Roosevelt have attempted to pack the Supreme Court?* There are many subsidiary problems as well, dividing themselves into evaluations of substantive issues and careful consideration of the relationships of means and ends. Had the esteemed justices of the Supreme Court correctly interpreted the Constitution, or had they knowingly or unconsciously slipped into the role of partisans of class interest? Was the New Deal program, in part held unconstitutional, a justifiable remedy for the serious economic and social results of the depression? Whether or not this New Deal was justified aside from legal ramifications, did it cross, run counter to, or threaten the "correct" meaning of the United States Constitution? When Congress, apparently representing a vast majority of the people, passes a program for economic reform, how far may interpretations by a slight majority of the Supreme Court defeat such a program?

Even should one hold the Roosevelt program was justifiable in a political sense, sound economically, and upon impeccable legal ground, the nature of Mr. Roosevelt's proposals for Court reform should be examined. Without engaging in the worthwhile, but sometimes trite prejudgment that good ends may be destroyed by the means employed, dispassionate and critical examination of the evidence should be sought concerning Mr. Roosevelt's remedies, popularly called "court packing." Did the evils exist? Are old judges usually incompetent? Was Roosevelt's scheme a proper prescription for Court reform; was it an unclean method — an immoral subterfuge of a power hungry administration?

Finally as time passes, as historical perspective is added, did the controversy precipitated by Mr. Roosevelt in his message of February 5, 1937, make permanently suspect the reputation of the Supreme Court, the Executive Departments, or the Congress?

In approaching this problem there are a few reference points which should be observed in relationship to the readings which follow.

In the dark economic shadows of 1933, and later, Mr. Roosevelt's administration and a compliant Congress initiated a number of programs involving new legislation and designed to mitigate and eventually end a depression. By the time Mr. Roosevelt's proposals for Court reform were a matter of public debate, the Supreme Court had declared its opinion upon several of these federal programs, usually adversely. On the contrary, it had treated state statutes somewhat more kindly. Decisions in the more important cases were as follows:

Federal Statutes	Action	Vote
Hot Oil	void	8–1
Gold Clauses	valid	5–4
Railroad Pensions	void	5–4
Farm Mortgages	void	9–0
N.R.A.	void	9–0
A.A.A.	void	6–3
T.V.A.	valid	8–1
Guffey Act	void	6–3
Municipal Bankruptcy	void	5–4

State Statutes		
Mortgage Moratorium	valid	5–4
Milk Price Act	valid	5–4
Minimum Wage	void	5–4

The selection from Carl B. Swisher's *American Constitutional Development* will serve as a clear and careful delineation of how the conflict developed between the New Deal and the Court. The published text of Mr. Roosevelt's message to Congress, the letter of the Attorney General, Homer S. Cummings, and the text of the law as originally proposed are presented to clarify the development of the plan.

For those interested in public reactions, there is a flavoring of editorial comment, in quantity preponderantly opposed to the plan, indeed just as the press preponderantly opposed the New Deal. The reader can compare his later readings with the quick sharp editorial attack in *The New York Herald-Tribune*, or the later, more detailed attack leveled at the proposals by *The New York Times*. Supporting Mr. Roosevelt, but indeed recognizing the gravity of the proposals, were statements from *The New Republic* and *The Nation*. An article, from which selections are taken, written after the defeat of the President's specific proposals, and which affords a more detached view of the struggle is Bernard DeVoto's "Desertion from the New Deal."

In finding and offering selections written at longer range, but perhaps with greater analytical intuition, one must select from rich materials and skeletonize the selections or the reader would be confounded by a profusion of worthwhile reading. In a long and able discussion, *The Supreme Court in United States History*, Charles Warren reviewed the history of the Supreme Court. Included here is the short summary of his two volume work. It epitomizes the attitude of those who defended the "nine old men" before 1933. Not all persons with historical curiosity, social observation, and facile pens agreed with Mr. Warren. The selection following Warren's judgment is in reality a part of a relatively longer, sustained attack upon alleged judicial blockade of democratic process contained in Max Lerner's *Ideas Are Weapons*. This, published in 1939, has the advantage of hindsight when it is compared with a part of Robert E. Cushman's *The Supreme Court and the Constitution*. Cushman on the whole favored the Court, and much of the value of his analysis arises from the very fact that he, in the year preceding Roosevelt's proposals, examined the basis of the controversy, drew conclusions, and suggested several different remedies.

In the bitterness of the struggle, both sides, by accident or design, maneuvered for the support of public opinion, the press, and particularly the members of the Senate. The Court itself, with the President's criticisms blowing hot upon it, reversed its traditional position on minimum wage laws, previously presented in *Adkins v. Children's Hospital*, by upholding a state law regulating wages in a new decision, *West Coast Hotel Company v. Parrish*. At the height of the controversy Justice Van Devanter, who voted with Mr. Roosevelt's opponents, resigned to the discomfiture of the proponents of the bill, since he thus reduced the urgency of the proposal. His status was discussed in the adverse report of the Senate Judiciary Committee — released on June 14, 1937. Facing defeat, but striving for victory, Senator Joseph T. Robinson championed an amendment on July 6 in the Senate which was designed to save the plan but limited the rate at which it could be put into effect. The amendment was defeated and viciously mauled in debate. Senator

Robinson died; some would say, as a result of his strenuous efforts to support the wishes of the President. In the end, the Senate which spoke with deep and sincere respect for Senator Robinson after he died, interred the court packing plan by recommitting it to committee on July 22. Thus the specific Roosevelt proposal was defeated, but Mr. Roosevelt was not defeated in many of the ends he sought.

Readers will find mention of many of these facts in the drastically edited selections from the adverse report of the Senate Judiciary Committee, from Senate debate involving Senators Robinson and Guffey for the proposals, Senators Wheeler and O'Mahoney against them. The final selections in this brief volume are designed to recall and depict the actual language and arguments of members of the Supreme Court itself. After one has read the selections from the decision in *Adkins v. Children's Hospital* (1923) and compared them with similar selections from *West Coast Hotel v. Parrish* (1937) he at least cannot say that the Court packing fight was shadowboxing, or that its solution was not fundamental to the future of America.

There are those who with deep interest would probe more deeply into the problem. For them there is a list of suggested readings at the end. But for both those who would read less or more, this volume will still serve to whet their curiosity. After all, *should* Roosevelt have tried to pack the Supreme Court?

[NOTE: The statements in the Clash of Issues on page ix by Maury Maverick and Senator William H. King are from "Should the President's Proposals Regarding the Supreme Court Be Adopted?" *America's Town Meeting of the Air*, Series II, Number 13 (New York, February 11, 1937), pp. 6 and 30.]

CONTENTS

THE CLASH OF ISSUES

In 1937 The New York Herald-Tribune commented:

It was a French King, Louis XIV, who said, "L'état, c'est moi" — "I am the State." The paper shell of American constitutionalism would continue if President Roosevelt secured the passage of the law he now demands. But it would be only a shell.

As the controversy grew, The Nation stated editorially:

While logically the plan is leaky, psychologically it is sound. For talk as we may about educating the common man on the judicial power, the thing that sticks in his mind is that the men who exercise it are old men and therefore probably behind the times.

As for Mr. Roosevelt, he declared:

In the uncertain state of the law, it is not difficult for the ingenious to devise novel reasons for attacking the validity of new legislation or its application. While these questions are laboriously brought to issue and debated through a series of courts, the government must stand aside. It matters not that the Congress has enacted the law, that the Executive has signed it and that the administrative machinery is waiting to function.

Debating on Town Meeting of the Air, Maury Maverick argued:

Why should a change be made in the High Court? Because our country is today a land of raging floods, of gigantic strikes, of millions of unemployed and economically insecure men and women, of farmers and business men who were all but destroyed by one depression and who dread the possibility of another.

The Supreme Court has knocked out almost everything the mass of the people want, and must have, if we are to survive as a democracy.

At the same time and place, Senator William H. King answered:

The present members of the Court have proven themselves to be men of character and faithful public servants. They have discharged the duties devolving upon them with courage and marked ability. They are competent in every way to fill with honor the high station which they occupy. Their work is current, and their capacity for service is unimpaired. To mutilate or emasculate the Court, in my opinion, can not be justified.

Carl Brent Swisher:

THE SUPREME COURT IN TRANSITION

"AFTER March 4, 1929," said Franklin D. Roosevelt in a campaign address in 1932, "the Republican party was in complete control of all branches of the federal government — the Executive, the Senate, the House of Representatives, and I might add for good measure, the Supreme Court as well." The reference to the Republicanism of the Supreme Court presumably had to do, not with party membership in a narrow sense, but with the identification of a majority of the Court with the conservative philosophy of government which the Republican party professed. The conservatism of four of the Justices, Van Devanter, McReynolds, Sutherland, and Butler, and the diligence with which they guarded rights of property against the extension of governmental control have been amply illustrated in earlier chapters. It will be recalled that Chief Justice Hughes and Justice Roberts seemed to occupy something of a middle ground, shifting back and forth between liberal and conservative positions. By comparison with their brethren, Justices Brandeis, Stone, and Cardozo could be classified as liberals. Unless positions hitherto staunchly maintained had been shaken by the depression, therefore, the antagonism of four justices toward the New-Deal program was to be assumed, the alignment of two others was highly uncertain, and only three offered any prospect of enthusiasm for the program. There was room for

doubt even as to these three. Justice Brandeis, for example, while a stalwart defender of so-called human rights when they came into conflict with property rights and an advocate of governmental intervention for the protection of human rights, was also critical of bigness in any form. His disapproval of the consolidation of wealth in units alleged to be too large for efficient administration did not preclude a corresponding disapproval of establishment of huge and unwieldy governmental organizations, even for New-Deal purposes.

Chief Justice Hughes and other members of the Court, furthermore, embodied the traditional distrust held by the judiciary and the bar for non-judicial administrative agencies to which the determination of rights had to be delegated if government was to perform broad regulatory and administrative functions. They knew the impracticability of treating as judicial questions all questions affecting rights and of requiring their determination by already overloaded judicial systems, but they retained the conviction that only the courts could be relied upon for a disciplined settlement of controversial questions. In an address delivered before the Federal Bar Association in February, 1931, Chief Justice Hughes called attention to the fact that overworked legislatures had been unable to keep pace with social demands and had adopted the practice, after the formula-

This selection from Carl Brent Swisher, *American Constitutional Development* (1943), pp. 920–943, is reprinted by permission of and arrangement with Houghton Mifflin Company, the authorized publishers.

tion of some very general standards, of turning over the business of regulation to a great variety of administrative agencies. The distinctive development of the era, he said, was one which raised the problem of executive justice, or administrative justice. A host of controversies as to provisional rights were now decided, not in the courts, but by administrators. Administrative authority within a constantly widening sphere of action, and subject only to the limitations of certain broad principles, established particular rules, found facts, and determined the limits of particular rights. This power was of enormous consequence. "An unscrupulous administrator might be tempted to say, 'Let me find the facts for the people of my country, and I care little who lays down the general principles.'" He admitted that this development had been to a great extent a necessary one, but declared that these new methods put us to new tests, "and the serious question of the future is whether we have enough of the old spirit which gave us our institutions to save them from being overwhelmed."

The distrust of Chief Justice Hughes for administrative determinations unchecked by the courts was revealed again less than two weeks later in his opinion in the important case of Crowell *v.* Benson. By an involved process of reasoning and in the face of a devastating dissent, he recaptured for the courts power to redetermine facts designated as "jurisdictional facts" previously determined by administrative agencies. Unfortunately, almost any set of facts involved in a case could be dragged into the category of jurisdictional facts. The decision was a long step backward in the movement to lighten the burden of the courts and relieve them of tasks they were not equipped to perform and to build up administrative agencies accustomed to responsibility and equipped for the performance of various kinds of tasks. It reflected the attitude of a Court unlikely to be sympathetic with the flowering-out of a host of new federal administrative agencies, manned by inexperienced personnel who, in the process of the extension of federal control over most of the economic order, were in many instances to take action limiting and shaping the rights of the people.

Judicial Review of the New Deal

For an appraisal of the relation of the courts to the New Deal, it is important to recall the atmosphere and attitudes of the early years of the period. In his inaugural address, President Roosevelt promised vigorous leadership in combating the ills of the depression crisis — "action, and action now." Under the spur of his driving enthusiasm Congress accepted from his hand and enacted a list of drastic and far-reaching measures with a speed unprecedented in American history. Hosts of enthusiastic followers rushed to Washington to aid in saving the nation from economic disaster. They were filled with a sense of mission and a scorn for precedent. New agencies were established, manned, and put into operation virtually overnight for the performance of functions not hitherto considered functions of the federal government at all. Supervision and coordination were wholly inadequate. Only zeal for the cause kept machinery moving with any semblance of order. The cause, however, in the face of a threat of economic ruin, was one on which all citizens of every philosophy could unite. For the moment, something approaching unity of sentiment prevailed.

Not much was heard about the Supreme Court as the vast program of the

New Deal got under way. Some doubts as to the constitutionality of parts of the program were hesitantly expressed. It was widely believed that the crisis would be over before the Supreme Court could have an opportunity to act, but some uneasiness was felt lest crippling injunctions be issued on constitutional grounds. "All you need to do to scare the wits out of any administration leader," said a news commentator, "is to creep up behind him and whisper, 'Injunction.'"

Enforcement during the early months was carried on largely by propaganda. Failure to obey New-Deal regulations resulted oftentimes in public sentiment damaging to the culprit's business. Withdrawal of the blue eagle, the stamp of conformity with the President's re-employment agreement and with NRA codes, was a penalty not lightly to be incurred. Scattered judicial decisions of the early period suggest that the courts moved along with the prevailing sentiments. Two decisions handed down early in 1934, indicated that the Supreme Court, in recognition of what Justice Brandeis, in a minority opinion in 1932, had called "an emergency more serious than war," was attempting to find constitutional bases for drastic regulations deemed necessary to meet crisis conditions. In a case dealing with what was called a mortgage moratorium, the Court upheld a Minnesota law severely limiting the rights of creditors. In a New York milk case it apparently abandoned much hitherto rigid doctrine on the subject of price-fixing. Both cases were decided in the face of unrelenting opposition from Justices Van Devanter, McReynolds, Sutherland, and Butler.

The mortgage-moratorium case dealt with an emergency statute enacted in Minnesota in 1933, to postpone foreclosure of mortgages at a time when fore-closures were being made or threatened on such a scale as to disrupt the whole social and economic fabric of the state. The act permitted courts of the state to postpone sales and extend the period in which mortgaged property might be redeemed, a reasonable income or rental being paid in the meantime to the holder. It was challenged as an unconstitutional impairment of the obligation of contracts. Justice Sutherland, as spokesman for the minority, found ample precedents to justify the challenge. A majority of the Court, however, speaking through Chief Justice Hughes, held the act constitutional. The Chief Justice did not go so far as to contend that a state might at all times interfere in this manner with contract rights. Nor did he contend that an emergency created new governmental power. "Emergency does not increase granted powers or remove or diminish the restrictions imposed upon power granted or reserved." But, "while emergency does not create power, emergency may furnish the occasion for the exercise of power." The constitutional provisions against the impairment of the obligation of contracts was limited by the restriction that a state continued to possess authority to safeguard the vital interests of its people, even though contracts were affected. The Court concluded that an emergency existed in Minnesota which furnished a proper occasion for the exercise of the reserved power of the state to protect the vital interests of the community. It found that the interference with contracts authorized under the Minnesota statute was legitimate under the circumstances. In so doing, the Court seemed by implication to pave the way for the removal of constitutional barriers against the great mass of governmental regulations deemed necessary for dealing with the crisis.

In the New York milk case the Court, speaking through Justice Roberts, upheld a state statute creating a milk-control board with power to fix minimum and maximum retail prices to be charged by stores to consumers of milk. Justice Roberts admitted that the milk industry was not a public utility, that it did not constitute a monopoly, and that it did not depend upon any public grant or franchise. Within the definition of the four dissenting members of the Court, it was not a "business affected with a public interest." The Court, in effect, discarded that conception, however, as a measure for determining whether prices might legitimately be fixed by government. It took the position that there was no closed category of businesses actually affected with a public interest and that, where the public interest required, prices as well as other aspects of a business were subject to regulation. The decision represented a sharp break with past decisions in this field.

All in all, the two current decisions justified optimism on the part of New-Dealers. It was to be remembered, however, that they were arrived at by votes of five to four, the narrowest of possible margins, and that they had to do with the interpretation of state laws rather than with broad federal statutes, resulting in the creation of a huge federal bureaucracy. Furthermore, even though the two statutes were upheld, the opinions were so carefully phrased that if conditions changed slightly, or if other statutes to be brought before the Court varied slightly from those already passed upon, the Court could easily shift its ground without reversing the decisions.

While economic conditions gradually improved, the complete recovery hoped for was not achieved. For a number of reasons, public sentiment in favor of the New-Deal program lost its unanimity. It was impossible to maintain indefinitely the emotional pitch which made possible the administration of the program. The enforcement of varied types of emergency regulations became more and more irksome, both to businessmen and to consumers. The unbalanced federal budget and the growing cost of the New-Deal program caused uneasiness. People began to wonder if the multifarious and oftentimes conflicting activities of the government had really been necessary for the achievement of such recovery as had been brought about or for such further improvement as seemed in prospect.

With the growth of doubts came a relaxation of the sentiment which made enforcement possible without resort to the courts. The administration, which had hitherto sought to avoid litigation, now began a search for good cases by which to demonstrate the constitutionality of New-Deal measures and the determination of the government to enforce these measures. The search for test cases disclosed in the records of the government the effects of haste in drafting legislation, executive orders, and codes, and in working out procedures. Every case considered as a possible means of determining the validity of the essential features of the administration program involved legal defects or embarrassing points which threw doubt on the wisdom of using it. One of the serious errors discovered was in the code of fair competition for administration of the petroleum industry. It will be recalled that the National Industrial Recovery Act gave the President power to modify the code. It seems that a change was ordered to be made in the petroleum code and that, in copying the document so as to include a new provision, the penalty provision of the code was inadvertently omitted, thereby leaving the code without any legal sanction whatsoever. The Petroleum Administration, unaware of or ignoring this highly important technical error, proceeded with the enforcement of the code as if penalties were still prescribed. In a case against one J. W. Smith, originally intended by the government as a test case for the National Industrial Recovery Act, it was discovered, in the language of counsel in a later case, that "Smith was arrested, indicted, and held in jail for several days and then had to put up bond for violating a law that did not exist."

Government counsel discovered the error and the case was dropped, for this or other reasons. Two other cases, of which one involved, not merely the petroleum code, but other provisions of the National Industrial Recovery Act dealing with regulation of the petroleum industry, were taken to the Supreme Court. Counsel for the private parties involved were able to embarrass government counsel in a discussion of the missing provision of the petroleum code; and members of the Court insisted on being told how codes and other executive orders were made available for the use of the government and of the public. It was disclosed that orders having the force of law were being issued at a rapid rate without any systematic mode of making them available. It was oftentimes next to impossible for private parties, and even government officials, to discover the content of the law on a given subject. From the bench and in its subsequent opinion, the Court criticized such disreputable procedure. The disclosures and the criticism had the important effect of bringing success to the movement for the publication of a magazine to be called the *Federal Register,* in which the great mass of orders having

the force of law were to be printed. The establishment of the *Federal Register* was followed by the codification of the mass of such orders as existed at that time.

The cases involved in the petroleum litigation, the so-called "hot-oil" cases, are remembered, however, not for their applicability to the petroleum code, but for the decision with respect to a provision in the National Industrial Recovery Act giving certain powers to the President. The provision authorized the President to prohibit the transportation in interstate and foreign commerce of petroleum produced in excess of the amount permitted by any state law or valid regulation. It did not attempt to guide the discretion of the President. He might prohibit shipment or not, as he saw fit. The President issued an executive order prohibiting the interstate or foreign shipment of "hot oil." With only Justice Cardozo dissenting, the Court held that the conferring of this power upon the President, without the prescription of a policy or standard to guide his decision, was an unconstitutional delegation of legislative power. Although the Court had often paid lip-service to the principle that legislative power could not be delegated, it had never before held a federal statute unconstitutional on that ground. Even though the damage done by this particular decision was easily curable by new legislation — which was speedily enacted — the step taken by the Court was ominous.

The next New-Deal cases to be decided were the so-called gold-clause cases. It will be recalled that all gold and gold certificates had been ordered turned in to the United States Treasury and that a joint resolution of Congress declared provisions in public and private contracts for payment in gold contrary to public policy and unenforceable in the courts of the United States. For the purpose of reviving business, the President exercised powers given by Congress to reduce the gold content of the dollar, or, in other words, to reduce the amount of gold by which the value of the dollar was to be measured. Public and private contracts then outstanding to the amount of several billions of dollars were affected. Price-levels were not greatly changed. Persons who by contract were entitled to payment in gold could purchase with devalued dollars almost as much in commodities as they could have purchased before the presidential order was issued. They suffered little or no loss by the action of the government, except for the fact that they, like other people, had to forego the right to gold. It was widely contended, however, that these persons had property rights in gold-clause contracts which could not be destroyed by legislation. If the government had the right to call all gold into the Treasury and to refuse to pay it out or to permit private individuals to use it in satisfaction of contracts, it was contended that gold-clause contracts made before the dollar was devalued could be satisfied only by the payment of an additional amount in devalued dollars corresponding to the extent of the devaluation. For example, a contract for payment of a dollar in gold could not be satisfied by a paper dollar representing only about fifty-nine cents as measured by the amount of gold held prior to devaluation.

The question was argued in terms of morals as well as of law. It was regarded as a particularly heinous offense for the federal government to flout its obligations in this manner. On the other hand, it was contended that the obligation to adjust the monetary system in such a way as to promote the welfare of all the people constituted a higher obligation than that to carry out in all their provisions the contracts for the payment of gold. Public contracts, like private contracts, were made subject to the limitation that the performance of their provisions must not be injurious to the public welfare. It was recognized, furthermore, that the national economy had been adjusted to the deflated currency, and that Supreme Court decisions requiring the fulfillment of gold-clause contracts with payments at face value plus amounts to the extent of the devaluation might result in financial chaos. This practical consideration may have had as much to do with the decisions of the Court as did its interpretation either of law or morality.

After keeping the cases under consideration over a period of weeks, during which the people waited tensely for a decision, the Supreme Court announced opinions in a series of gold-clause cases. The government was the victor by the narrowest of margins. In the first of the cases decided, Chief Justice Hughes, speaking for a majority of the Court, pointed out that the use of gold was closely related to the exercise of important powers which the Constitution conferred upon Congress. Contracts made between private parties could not restrain the exercise of powers, monetary or otherwise, possessed by Congress.

Contracts, however express, cannot fetter the constitutional authority of the Congress. Contracts may create rights of property, but when contracts deal with a subject matter which lies within the control of the Congress, they have a congenital infirmity. Parties cannot remove their transactions from the reach of dominant constitutional power by making contracts about them.[1]

[1] Norman v. Baltimore & Ohio Railroad Co., 294 U. S. 240 (1935).

The Court held that, in exercising its control over gold, Congress had acted within its powers and that private contracts could not be enforced in so far as they were inconsistent with that policy.

The Supreme Court also found that the holder of gold certificates who was required to surrender them to the government for their dollar value in spite of the allegedly high market value of gold was not entitled to further reimbursement from the government, since the certificates were only for gold dollars, and not for gold bullion. Finally, it held unconstitutional the repudiation of gold-clause contracts in United States bonds — giving Chief Justice Hughes an opportunity to scold the administration for the immorality of its conduct — but five justices agreed that the person bringing the suit had lost nothing by the devaluation process, and was therefore not entitled to sue.

The outcome was that the government won technical, though marginal, victories in all cases. Justice Stone wrote a concurring opinion in one case, and four justices joined in an indignant dissenting opinion written by Justice McReynolds to apply to all cases. In delivering his opinion in the courtroom he added extemporaneously the ominous statement, "As for the Constitution, it does not seem too much to say that it is gone."

The reaction of administration leaders to the gold-clause decisions was a mixture of relief and indignation. Although not quite believing that the Supreme Court would take the risk of creating the economic chaos that might result from adverse decisions, they had been anxiously searching for methods of softening the blow if it came. To protect the government against suits on its own gold-clause contracts, they had been planning legislation to withdraw the jurisdiction of federal courts to entertain such suits.

Even if they had succeeded in this field, however, the effect as to private contracts would have been disastrous. The five-to-four vote of the Court was too close for comfort; and they resented what they regarded as a moral lecture on the part of Chief Justice Hughes with reference to the repudiation of government contracts. It stood to reason that if some of the justices had been virtually coerced into supporting the government against their convictions, because of the disastrous effects which would have resulted from decisions of a different kind, their indignation at New-Deal methods would carry over to the decision of other cases where the results of adverse action would be less dangerous. Even though they had won a technical victory in the gold-clause suits against the government, administration leaders deemed it expedient to bring about the enactment of legislation to cut off additional suits of the kind in the near future. In the meantime, they turned to the defense of the program at points of greater vulnerability.

Judicial Disasters for the New Deal

Since late in 1933 a case, known as United States *v.* Belcher, had been pending in the courts and had been considered by government officials from time to time as satisfactory for use as a test case on code administration under the National Industrial Recovery Act. In response to criticism of the administration for failure to bring about the settlement of the question before the Supreme Court, the public at large and lower federal courts throughout the country were assured that this case, which involved administration of the lumber code, would bring about a definitive judicial test of the recovery statute. After the adverse decision of the Supreme Court in the oil cases, however, the Belcher case seemed exceedingly vulnerable. The government victory in the gold-clause cases was not of such a nature as to build confidence. On April 1, 1935, on the request of Solicitor General Stanley Reed, the Supreme Court dismissed the appeal. As a result, the administration was criticized for bad faith and was accused of admitting tacitly that it doubted the validity of legislation it was seeking to enforce.

In the meantime, without much publicity and evidently without the knowledge of many government officials interested in demonstrating the constitutionality of the National Industrial Recovery Act, government counsel had won, in lower federal courts in New York City, a criminal case that had arisen in connection with the administration of the poultry code. Had the government lost the case in the circuit court of appeals, there would have been no question of an appeal to the Supreme Court and of the use of this case as a test case for the recovery statute before the Supreme Court. When the defeated defendant petitioned for a Supreme Court review, however, the Department of Justice could do little more than make the best of the situation, even though, from a number of angles, the case was a bad one in which to present code administration in its best light.

The so-called live-poultry code applied only to an area in and around New York City in the states of New York, Connecticut, and New Jersey. It regulated hours, wages, and working conditions and various trade practices in the handling and slaughtering of poultry. Although most of the poultry sold in New York City came from states other than New York, the matters regulated seemed, on their face, to be largely local in character. The marketing of diseased and uninspected poultry was forbidden. Buyers were also forbidden to make selections among

fowls in particular coops instead of taking them as they came. The purpose of the latter provision was to prevent the practice whereby firstcomers selected the best poultry at the market price, whereafter price-cutting, which was of course injurious to the industry and therefore contrary to the purposes of the National Industrial Recovery Act, was necessary to dispose of the remaining, less desirable stock. The administration of these provisions, however, on which the constitutionality of the code structure of the National Industrial Recovery Act was to depend, was discussed in the courtroom in high levity. In response to a question from the bench, counsel for the poultry firm involved explained that "straight killing," which was required by the code, meant, "You have got to put your hand in the coop and take out whichever chicken comes to you." Thereafter the following colloquy took place:

"And it was for that your client was convicted?" asked Mr. Justice McReynolds.

"Yes, and fined and given a jail sentence," Mr. Heller replied.

"But if a customer wants half a coop of chickens, he has to take it just like it is," he further explained.

"What if the chickens are all at one end?" inquired Mr. Justice Sutherland. Counsel's answer to that question was lost in the laughter from the bench and the bar which ensued.

As to the charge of selling diseased poultry, Mr. Heller explained that it was based upon the sale of one chicken which had passed federal inspection, but which, upon an autopsy, was found to be "eggbound."

Amid the unfavorable atmosphere indicated, a government counsel had the task of persuading the Court that authorizing the President to make or sanction the rules enforced in the poultry industry did not represent an unconstitutional delegation of legislative power, that the rules constituted legitimate regulations of interstate commerce, and that they did not take liberty or property without due process of law.

The case, known as the Schechter case, or, more informally, as the "sick-chicken" case, was decided on May 27, 1935. Speaking for a unanimous Court, Chief Justice Hughes held that Section 3 of the recovery statute, which authorized the government of industry through codes of fair competition, was unconstitutional because of the sweeping delegation of legislative power. . . .

Justice Cardozo, the only justice who had dissented in the hot-oil case in which the Supreme Court first exercised its veto on the ground of the unconstitutional delegation of legislative power, concurred vigorously in the Schechter case. He said:

The delegated power of legislation which has found expression in this code is not canalized within banks that keep it from overflowing. It is unconfined and vagrant. . . . Here . . . is an attempted delegation not confined to any single act nor to any class or group of acts identified or described by reference to a standard. Here in effect is a roving commission to inquire into evils and upon discovery correct them.

Government by means of codes of fair competition was very different, he declared, from action against unfair methods of competition, such as that taken by the Federal Trade Commission. Delegation of the power to discover and denounce unfair practices was obviously necessary in view of the number and diversity of the industries of the country. Government by codes of fair competition went much farther:

It is to include whatever ordinances may be desirable or helpful for the well-being or prosperity of the industry affected. In that view, the function of its adoption is not merely negative, but positive; the planning of improvements as well as the extirpation of abuses. What is fair, as thus conceived, is not something to be contrasted with what is unfair or fraudulent or tricky. The extension becomes as wide as the field of industrial regulation. If that conception shall prevail, anything that Congress may do within the limits of the commerce clause for the betterment of business may be done by the President upon the recommendation of a trade association by calling it a code. This is delegation running riot. No such plenitude of power is susceptible of transfer. The statute, however, aims at nothing less, as one can learn both from its terms and from the administrative practice under it.

The Court also held unanimously that the practices involved in this case were in intrastate commerce and could not be regulated under the commerce clause. Government counsel had contended that the abuses to be prevented had such an injurious effect upon interstate commerce as to justify federal regulation. Drawing a distinction between direct and indirect effects upon interstate commerce, the Court rejected the contention.

The devastating result of the decision was that the statutory base, not merely for the poultry code, but for all codes formed under the National Industrial Recovery Act, was destroyed. Furthermore, the interstate-commerce aspect of the decision stood in the way of enforcement of important provisions in this and other codes, even if the codes should be submitted directly to Congress and enacted by it. The complete collapse of recovery machinery for the control of industry was decreed. The President told a press conference that the implications of this decision were probably more important than any decision since the Dred Scott case. From reading the decision he thought that the delegation of power was not an unsurmountable object, and that an act could be written giving definite directions to administrative or quasi-judicial bodies which would be acceptable. He regarded as more serious the narrow interpretation of the commerce clause. Although the country had been in "the horse-and-buggy age" when the commerce clause was written, the tendency in recent years had been to view the clause in the light of present-day civilization. He intimated that the Schechter decision represented a return to the horse-and-buggy age.

Two other important cases were decided against the administration on the day on which the Schechter case was decided. In one of them the Supreme Court held a federal farm-bankruptcy statute unconstitutional as taking the property of creditors without due process of law. In the other case, the Court held that the President had no power to remove a member of the Federal Trade Commission other than as prescribed in the Federal Trade Commission Act.

Three weeks earlier, while these cases were awaiting decision, Justice Roberts had joined the four traditional conservatives to make the majority of the Court which wrecked a comprehensive retirement scheme for railroad workers. The federal statute involved was perhaps not an integral part of the New-Deal program, but it was closely related to it. It was intended to provide economic security in old age for one class of workers, and it might have reduced the excess of workers seeking employment on railroads by providing a mode of subsistence for those beyond a certain age who had rendered service in earlier years. The Court not only found defects in this particular law, however, but decided the case in such a way as apparently to invalidate

any similar scheme sponsored by the federal government. On the whole, in spite of victories for the administration in the gold-clause cases, the 1934–1935 term of the Supreme Court made the prospect for drastic social legislation of any kind seem dismal indeed.

The 1935–1936 Term

The New Deal continued to suffer at the hands of the Supreme Court at the term beginning in October, 1935. In United States *v.* Butler, the processing-tax provisions of the Agricultural Adjustment Act, on which a major portion of the farm program was based, were held unconstitutional by a vote of six to three. Justice Roberts spoke for the Court in a complicated and mystifying opinion. He admitted that Congress had the power to tax in order to provide for the general welfare and to appropriate the money raised for that purpose. He did not deny the obvious fact that huge sums in revenue were raised by the processing tax. He did not deny that the taxing device might be used for regulatory purposes, if the purposes themselves were within the power of the federal government. A tax, however, he said, "in the general understanding of the term, and as used in the Constitution, signifies an exaction for the support of the government. The word has never been thought to connote the expropriation of money from one group for the benefit of another." The tax here provided for was not a means of raising revenue for support of the government, but was part of a plan to regulate and control agricultural production, "a matter beyond the powers delegated to the federal government." He rejected the contention that the plan was not compulsory. The farmer, of course, might refuse to comply, but the price of such refusal was the loss of benefits. "The amount offered is intended to be sufficient to exert pressure on him to agree to the proposed regulation. The power to confer or withhold unlimited benefits is the power to coerce or destroy."

In a dissenting opinion concurred in by Justices Brandeis and Cardozo, Justice Stone by implication accused his colleague of resorting to "a tortured construction of the Constitution," and remarked, "Courts are not the only agency of government that must be assumed to have capacity to govern." His words had influence, however, only in connection with the later attack upon the rigid conservatism of the Supreme Court. Control of agricultural production by the processing-tax device was invalidated for the time being, and it was clear that more obviously compulsory measures for limiting the production of cotton, tobacco, and potatoes were likewise unconstitutional. The statutes in question were accordingly repealed.

Another important decision turned on the constitutionality of the Bituminous Coal Conservation Act of 1935, a statute providing for the control of working conditions in the mining industry and for the fixing of prices for the sale of coal. Congress had been slow in passing the measure, justifying hesitancy on the ground that the constitutionality of such regulations was in doubt. The President sent to the subcommittee in charge of the bill a statement justifying the legislation. He closed with the following significant paragraph:

Manifestly, no one is in a position to give assurance that the proposed act will withstand constitutional tests, for the simple fact that you can get not ten but one thousand different legal opinions on the subject. But the situation is so urgent and the benefits of the legislation so evident that all doubts should be resolved in favor of the bill, leaving to the courts, in an orderly fashion, the ultimate question of constitutionality. A decision by the Supreme Court relative to this measure would be helpful as indicating with increasing clarity the constitutional limits within which this government must operate. The proposed bill has been carefully drafted by employers and employees working cooperatively. An opportunity should be given to the industry to attempt to work out some of its major problems. I hope your committee will not permit doubts as to constitutionality, however reasonable, to block the suggested legislation.

Opponents of the bill denounced the request of the President for enactment of the legislation in spite of doubts as to constitutionality, "however reasonable." They denounced the cavalier attitude of a President who would advocate legislation without reference to constitutional difficulties, leaving their solution to the Supreme Court. They quoted with approval from a veto message in which President Taft had taken an entirely different attitude. . . .

The Roosevelt statement, however, was written in the knowledge that constitutional arguments were being used against the bill when the real reasons for opposition had little or nothing to do with the Constitution. Furthermore, it seemed to the administration that the Supreme Court, under the cover of interpreting the Constitution, was making itself the arbiter of governmental policy in rivalry with the elected representatives of the people. Rather than to yield passively to judicial opposition to New-Deal policies, officials deemed it better strategy to require the Court to show its hand in as many cases as possible, thereby demonstrating to the people that the Court, and not the administration, was responsible for the ineffectiveness of the program. The act was passed, and the

Court responded by its decision in Carter *v.* Carter Coal Company.

Dividing on different points by votes of six to three and five to four, it held the act unconstitutional. The majority opinion, written by Justice Sutherland, reflected throughout a narrow conception of the powers of the federal government. He argued:

The proposition, often advanced and as often discredited, that the power of the federal government inherently extends to purposes affecting the nation as a whole with which the states severally cannot deal or cannot adequately deal, and the related notion that Congress, entirely apart from those powers delegated by the Constitution, may enact laws to promote the general welfare, have never been accepted, but always definitely rejected, by this Court.

Federal authority under the statute was supported by means of a taxing device. An excise tax was levied in such a way as to operate as a penalty upon those producers of coal who failed to comply with the provisions of the act. The constitutional basis for the regulatory provisions of the statute, however, had to be found, not in the taxing power, but in the commerce power. Justice Sutherland analyzed the word "commerce" to show that it was the equivalent of the phrase "intercourse for the purposes of trade." Plainly, he said, the incidents leading up to and culminating in the mining of coal did not constitute such intercourse. The employment of workers in mining was not interstate commerce. It might have an effect upon such commerce, but the effect was indirect, however great its magnitude, and was therefore not subject to federal control. The conclusion that working conditions were obviously local conditions over which the federal government had no legislative control implied

so drastic a curtailment of the commerce power as to threaten the enforcement of other important measures by which the administration sought to restore order in the field of industrial relations and improve the conditions of labor.

Justice Sutherland found also that legislative power was unconstitutionally delegated in the provisions of the statute whereby maximum hours of labor were to be determined by certain percentages of the producers in the industry. He found that provisions as to hours and wages did not accord with the requirement of due process of law. Having held that the labor provisions were defective, he reached the further conclusion that the price-fixing provisions in the statute could not stand alone and that the entire act must be held unconstitutional and void. Justice Cardozo wrote a vigorous dissenting opinion, concurred in by Justices Brandeis and Stone, which served further to portray the majority of the Court as an agency setting out deliberately to use constitutional interpretation as an instrument to curb distasteful governmental policies.

Other federal statutes suffered a similar fate. By a vote of five to four, with Justice McReynolds as spokesman for the majority, the Court invalidated the Municipal Bankruptcy Act of 1934. In an important case involving administrative procedure in connection with the fixing of stockyard rates by the Secretary of Agriculture, Chief Justice Hughes, for a majority of the Court, reasserted the power of the judiciary to inquire into facts already determined by the administrator when constitutional questions turned upon them. When the constitutionality of a regulation depended upon such matters as net income and valuation, even though these matters were essentially factual, the Court held that they were subject to re-examination. The effect of the decision was to broaden the judicial authority over fact-finding previously asserted in Crowell *v.* Benson in connection with so-called jurisdictional facts. In another case the Court limited the power thought to have been given to the Securities and Exchange Commission.

A decision having to do with the establishment of minimum wages for women, although it concerned a state statute, was regarded also as a New-Deal defeat. In the Adkins case, decided in 1923, the Supreme Court had held that Congress had no power to prescribe minimum wages for women in the District of Columbia. By a vote of five to four, with Justice Roberts joining the conservatives and Justice Butler speaking for the majority, the Court held that the decision as to a New York law must follow the earlier decision. The reasoning stood in the way of new federal legislation that might attempt to eliminate the evil of substandard wages.

The administration achieved only one important victory at the term of the Court under discussion. With only Justice McReynolds dissenting, the Court upheld the constitutional power of the federal government to dispose of electric power generated at Wilson Dam in the Tennessee Valley. Chief Justice Hughes emphasized the relation to the war power and to the power of Congress to improve the navigability of streams as an incident to the regulation of commerce. He emphasized also the power of the federal government "to dispose of and make all needful rules and regulations respecting the territory or other property belonging to the United States."

In a sense, the TVA decision, nominally the one bright spot in the Supreme Court record for the term, constituted an embarrassment for the administration. It indicated that the Court had not set out maliciously to batter every major feature of the New-Deal program, and that, if New-Deal legislation could be brought within the traditional lines of constitutional interpretation, it might be upheld by the Court. In spite of the conviction of many administration leaders that the Court had set out deliberately to sabotage their program, the lineup of decisions conveyed the suggestion that it was the program and not the Court that was wrong. Presumably no administration leaders accepted this interpretation, but a number of them realized the persuasiveness of the argument as far as the general public was concerned.

The Attempt at Judicial Reform

In any event, the prospects remained gloomy for the portions of the New-Deal program not yet passed upon. These included such major statutes as the National Labor Relations Act, the Social Security Act, and the Public Utility Holding Company Act. Furthermore, the replacement of some of the statutes invalidated was being planned, along with the enactment of new measures of social significance. It appeared that something would have to be done about the Supreme Court if such enactments were to constitute anything more than futile gestures.

A device much discussed, and actually employed to a limited extent, was to withdraw the jurisdiction of federal courts to entertain suits of a kind likely to embarrass the government. Since the government could not be sued without its own consent, it was an easy matter to secure the enactment of legislation cutting off suits against the government by persons contending that they had been injured by the devaluation of the currency. The device was used again in connection with suits against the government to recover taxes unconstitutionally collected under the Agricultural Adjustment Act of 1933. Such suits were to be entertained by the courts only if the persons bringing them could prove, not only that they had paid the taxes, but that they had not either passed them back to farmers in the form of lower prices paid for raw materials or forward to consumers in the form of higher prices.

Further limitations of jurisdiction were under constant discussion as a means of preventing judicial interference with the New-Deal program, but it was practically impossible to withdraw all constitutional questions from judicial determination. As to the original jurisdiction of the Supreme Court, indeed, it was derived, not from Congress, but from the Constitution itself. Even if, as was not generally believed, the appellate jurisdiction of the Supreme Court could be cut off in cases involving constitutional questions, those questions must inevitably be raised in the lower federal courts. Many of those courts showed a disapproval of the New-Deal program no less ardent than that of the Supreme Court. Furthermore, the disparity of decisions on constitutional questions, if not subject to the unifying influence of the Supreme Court, would result in chaos throughout the several judicial districts.

Constitutional amendments to clear the way for New-Deal measures were also considered. The amending device was opposed because of the difficulty and the time to be consumed in securing amendments. Furthermore, although the Supreme Court was at times unanimous or close to unanimous in its position, a number of decisions made the cleavage among the justices sharply apparent, and suggested that the remedy lay with the Court and not with the Constitution. In

May, 1935, after the decision on the Railroad Retirement Act, Attorney General Homer Cummings included the following comment in a letter to the President:

The case was always a difficult one, but the form the opinions took would seem to indicate such a marked cleavage in the Supreme Court that it may be, and probably is, a forecast of what we may expect with reference to almost any form of social legislation that Congress may enact. Apparently there are at least four justices who are against any attempt to use the power of the federal government for bettering general conditions, except within the narrowest limitations. This is a terrific handicap and brings up again, rather acutely, matters we have previously discussed, including a proposed constitutional amendment.

The Attorney General continued to watch the situation and to analyze the possibilities of constitutional amendments and of congressional limitations on the jurisdiction of the Supreme Court. The real difficulty, he wrote to the President in January, 1936, was not with the Constitution, but with the judges who interpreted it. As long as a majority of those who had the final say in such matters were wedded to their present theories, there were but two courses open. The administration must endeavor to find a way to bring helpful national legislation within the explicit terms of the decisions being reached by the Court or it must frankly meet the issue of a constitutional amendment. For the present he preferred the former course. He said:

If we come to the question of a constitutional amendment, enormous difficulties are presented. No one has yet suggested an amendment that does not do either too much or too little, or which does not raise practical and political questions which it would be better to avoid. If we had liberal judges, with a lively sense of the importance of the social problems which have now spilled over state lines, there would be no serious difficulties; and the existing constitutional restraint when interpreted by such a Court would be very salutary.

He suggested giving serious thought to a constitutional amendment which would require the retirement of all federal judges, or at least all Supreme Court judges, at the age of seventy. It would have the advantage of not changing in the least degree the structure of the government; nor would it impair the power of the Court. It would merely insure the exercise of the powers of the Court by judges less likely to be horrified by new ideas.

During the presidential campaign of 1936, Republicans and such non-partisan or bi-partisan organizations as the Liberty League lauded the Supreme Court as the defender of the rights of the people against New-Deal encroachments. The President, on the other hand, made no public comment about the Republicanism of the Supreme Court, such as he had made four years earlier, avoiding all attacks upon that institution which might create public antagonism. The administration sought to fix the attention of voters upon its program and not upon governmental machinery. All who thought deeply about the subject knew that for the preservation of the program something would have to be done about the judicial blockade, but most of them were willing to leave the mode of action to future determination.

In the meantime, the office of the solicitor general was secretly making a comprehensive study of the various suggestions, "by which the legislature might, to a greater or lesser extent, lessen its vulnerability to the constitutional views of a majority of the Court." The study was made, said the solicitor general in a memorandum for the Attorney General on December 19, 1936, "so that if, as, and when the President brings the matter up again, we would have this background. It was suggested at the first cabinet meeting after the election that we should be thinking on them."

The study analyzed, classified, and appraised the various suggestions having some element of feasibility. The suggestions included the following: Congress should insist on determining such facts as whether a given industry or practice had a direct effect upon interstate commerce; through its control over procedure, Congress should require that the vote necessary to invalidate an act be more than a bare majority of the Court; Congress should withdraw from the jurisdiction of the lower federal courts, and from the appellate jurisdiction of the Supreme Court, the power to pass upon the constitutionality of acts of Congress; the membership of the Supreme Court might be increased to allow the appointment of enough liberal justices to insure a majority; and finally, Congress might adjust retirement compensation progressively so as to make retirement at seventy or at a similarly early age much more attractive than in the later years of life.

From the point of view of the general history of the period, the document was significant. As background for the action taken soon after it was written, however, it served chiefly to clear the air by pointing out impossibilities or pitfalls in the way of achieving the desired ends. The writer or writers were extremely pessimistic about the practicability of any of the proposals, when both legal and political objections were taken into account.

The Court Fight

Around the turn of the year 1936–1937, the President and the Attorney General agreed on the outlines of a plan. Without again taking up the subject with his cabinet, the President consulted with the Attorney General from time to time, as the program was worked out with great secrecy in the Department of Justice. Since the difficulty was not with the Constitution, but was with the Court, they agreed that a constitutional amendment was not the appropriate remedy. Both knew, furthermore, that, although the President had carried all but two states in the recent election, as many as thirteen states might fail to sanction a constitutional amendment, in which event the amendment would not become operative.

They concluded that the subject must be dealt with in terms of the retirement of aged justices or the superseding of such justices. Since under the Constitution the justices served during good behavior, there was no way to compel them to retire merely on grounds of age. The device hit upon, therefore, was to assume that justices over seventy years of age were to some extent incompetent and provide for the appointment of an additional justice for each justice who had served for ten years and had not resigned or retired within six months after reaching the age of seventy. The plan was not novel. It was already in effect with respect to circuit and district judges, except that there had to be a finding of mental or physical disability of a permanent character. Its automatic operation in the Supreme Court would have been humiliating to the justices involved, however, and might in fact have coerced them into retirement. Presumably, the President and the Attorney General hoped for such an outcome. If the aged justices did not retire, it was hoped that their conservative votes would be outnumbered by majorities including the votes of the new appointees.

With the mode of attack agreed upon, the sponsors were faced with a further problem of strategy. Should the attack be made with its purpose starkly apparent — the purpose of reversing the trend of Supreme Court decisions on New-Deal measures, or should the issue be merged with issues of other needed judicial reforms? The records of the purely political arguments on this subject are not yet available. This much is known, however. Attorney General Cummings was deeply interested in a whole series of reforms in the federal court system. To him the fact that justices well beyond the retirement age, and out of touch with the problems of the nation, retained Supreme Court positions to the detriment of the public welfare, provided only one example of the antiquated character of the system. He knew that procedure was excessively complicated, that the several federal courts were poorly co-ordinated for the disposition of the judicial burden and for handling the business matters of the courts themselves, and that many positions on the lower federal courts were occupied by men who could fairly be characterized as "dead wood." The problem as he saw it was not simply one of packing the Supreme Court to get specific New-Deal measures held constitutional, but was rather one of renovating the judiciary as a whole. Presumably it was largely on the basis of his persuasion that the attack was made in terms of the aggregate of needed reforms, rather than simply in terms of changing the membership of the Supreme Court.

The President submitted the plan for judicial reform to Congress on February 5, 1937. . . .

TEXTS OF THE PROPOSALS

FEBRUARY 6, 1937

Following are the text of the President's message to Congress on the judiciary, the draft of his proposed law, and the text of the letter of Attorney General Cummings to the President.

A. ROOSEVELT'S COURT MESSAGE, *Washington*, February 5, 1937

I HAVE recently called the attention of the Congress to the clear need for a comprehensive program to reorganize the administrative machinery of the executive branch of our government. I now make a similar recommendation to the Congress in regard to the judicial branch of the Government, in order that it also may function in accord with modern necessities.

The Constitution provides that the President "shall from time to time give to the Congress information of the state of the Union, and recommend to their consideration such measures as he shall judge necessary and expedient." No one else is given a similar mandate. It is therefore the duty of the President to advise the Congress in regard to the judiciary whenever he deems such information or recommendation necessary.

I address you for the further reason that the Constitution vests in the Congress direct responsibility in the creation of courts and judicial offices and in the formulation of rules of practice and procedure. It is, therefore, one of the definite duties of the Congress constantly to maintain the effective functioning of the Federal judiciary.

The judiciary has often found itself handicapped by insufficient personnel with which to meet a growing and more complex business. It is true that the physical facilities of conducting the business of the courts have been greatly improved, in recent years, through the erection of suitable quarters, the provision of adequate libraries and the addition of subordinate court officers. But in many ways these are merely the trappings of judicial office. They play a minor part in the processes of justice.

Since the earliest days of the republic, the problem of the personnel of the courts has needed the attention of the Congress. For example, from the beginning, over repeated protests to President Washington, the justices of the Supreme Court were required to "ride circuit" and, as circuit justices, to hold trials throughout the length and breadth of the land – a practice which endured over a century.

In almost every decade since 1789, changes have been made by the Congress whereby the numbers of judges and the duties of judges in Federal Courts have been altered in one way or another. The Supreme Court was established with six members in 1789; it was reduced to five in 1801; it was increased to seven in 1807; it was increased to nine in 1837; it was increased to ten in 1863; it was reduced to seven in 1866; it was increased to nine in 1869.

The simple fact is that today a new need for legislative action arises because the personnel of the Federal judiciary is insufficient to meet the business before them. A growing body of our citizens complain of the complexities, the delays, and the expense of litigation in United States courts.

A letter from the Attorney General, which I submit herewith, justifies by reasoning and statistics the common impression created by our overcrowded Federal dockets — and it proves the need for additional judges.

Delay in any court results in injustice. It makes lawsuits a luxury available only to the few who can afford them or who have property interests to protect which are sufficiently large to repay the cost. Poorer litigants are compelled to abandon valuable rights or to accept inadequate or unjust settlements because of sheer inability to finance or to await the end of a long litigation. Only by speeding up the processes of the law and thereby reducing their cost, can we eradicate the growing impression that the courts are chiefly a haven for the well-to-do.

Delays in the determination of appeals have the same effect. Moreover, if trials of original actions are expedited and existing accumulations of cases are reduced, the volume of work imposed on the Circuit Courts of Appeal will further increase.

The attainment of speedier justice in the courts below will enlarge the task of the Supreme Court itself. And still more work would be added by the recommendation which I make later in this message for the quicker determination of constitutional questions by the highest court.

Even at the present time the Supreme Court is laboring under a heavy burden. Its difficulties in this respect were superficially lightened some years ago by authorizing the court, in its discretion, to refuse to hear appeals in many classes of cases. This discretion was so freely exercised that in the last fiscal year, although 867 petitions for review were presented to the Supreme Court, it declined to hear 717 cases.

If petitions in behalf of the government are excluded, it appears that the court permitted private litigants to prosecute appeals in only 108 cases out of 803 applications. Many of the refusals were doubtless warranted. But can it be said that full justice is achieved when a court is forced by the sheer necessity of keeping up with its business to decline, without even an explanation, to hear 87 per cent of the cases presented to it by private litigants?

It seems clear, therefore, that the necessity of relieving present congestion extends to the enlargement of the capacity of all the Federal courts.

A part of the problem of obtaining a sufficient number of judges to dispose of cases is the capacity of the judges themselves. This brings forward the question of aged or infirm judges — a subject of delicacy and yet one which requires frank discussion.

In the Federal courts there are in all 237 life tenure permanent judgeships. Twenty-five of them are now held by judges over 70 years of age and eligible to leave the bench on full pay. Originally no pension or retirement allowance was provided by the Congress.

When after eighty years of our national history the Congress made provision for pensions, it found a well-entrenched tradition among judges to cling to their posts, in many instances far beyond their years of physical or mental capacity. Their salaries were small. As with other men, responsibilities and obligations accumulated. No alternative had been open to them except to attempt to perform the duties of their offices to the very edge of the grave.

In exceptional cases, of course, judges, like other men, retain to an advanced age full mental and physical vigor. Those not so fortunate are often unable to perceive their own infirmities. "They seem to be tenacious of the appearance of adequacy." The Voluntary Retirement Law of 1869 provided, therefore, only a partial solution. That law, still in force, has not proved effective in inducing aged judges to retire on a pension.

This result had been foreseen in the debates when the measure was being considered. It was then proposed that when a judge refused to retire upon reaching the age of 70, an additional judge should be appointed to assist in the work of the court. The proposal passed the House, but was eliminated in the Senate.

With the opening of the twentieth century, and the great increase of population and commerce, and the growth of a more complex type of litigation, similar proposals were introduced in the Congress. To meet the situation, in 1913, 1914, 1915 and 1916, the Attorneys General then in office recommended to the Congress that when a district or a circuit judge failed to retire at the age of 70, an additional judge be appointed in order that the affairs of the court might be promptly and adequately discharged.

In 1919 a law was finally passed providing that the President "may" appoint additional district and circuit judges, but only upon a finding that the incumbent judge over 70 "is unable to discharge efficiently all the duties of his office by reason of mental or physical disability of permanent character." The discretionary and indefinite nature of this legislation

has rendered it ineffective. No President should be asked to determine the ability or disability of any particular judge.

The duty of a judge involves more than presiding or listening to testimony or arguments. It is well to remember that the mass of details involved in the average of law cases today is vastly greater and more complicated than even twenty years ago. Records and briefs must be read; statutes, decisions and extensive material of a technical, scientific, statistical and economic nature must be searched and studied; opinions must be formulated and written. The modern tasks of judges call for the use of full energies.

Modern complexities call also for a constant infusion of new blood in the courts, just as it is needed in executive functions of the government and in private business. A lowered mental or physical vigor leads men to avoid an examination of complicated and changed conditions. Little by little, new facts become blurred through old glasses fitted, as it were, for the needs of another generation; older men, assuming that the scene is the same as it was in the past, cease to explore or inquire into the present or the future.

We have recognized this truth in the civil service of the nation and of many States by compelling retirement on pay at the age of 70. We have recognized it in the army and navy by retiring officers at the age of 64. A number of States have recognized it by providing in their Constitutions for compulsory retirement of aged judges.

Life tenure of judges, assured by the Constitution, was designed to place the courts beyond temptations or influences which might impair their judgments; it was not intended to create a static judiciary. A constant and systematic addition of younger blood will vitalize the courts and better equip them to recognize and apply the essential concepts of justice in the light of the needs and the facts of an ever-changing world.

It is obvious, therefore, from both reason and experience, that some provision must be adopted, which will operate automatically to supplement the work of older judges and accelerate the work of the courts.

I, therefore, earnestly recommend that the necessity of an increase in the number of judges be supplied by legislation providing for the appointment of additional judges in all Federal courts, without exception, where there are incumbent judges of retirement age who do not choose to retire or to resign. If an elder judge is not in fact incapacitated, only good can come from the presence of an additional judge in the crowded state of the dockets; if the capacity of an elder judge is in fact impaired, the appointment of an additional judge is indispensable. This seems to be a truth which cannot be contradicted.

I also recommend that the Congress provide machinery for taking care of sudden or long-standing congestion in the lower courts. The Supreme Court should be given power to appoint an administrative assistant who may be called a proctor. He would be charged with the duty of watching the calendars and the business of all the courts in the Federal system. The Chief Justice thereupon should be authorized to make a temporary assignment of any circuit or district judge hereafter appointed in order that he may serve as long as needed in any circuit or district where the courts are in arrears.

I attach a carefully considered draft of a proposed bill, which, if enacted, would, I am confident, afford substantial relief.

The proposed measure also contains a limit on the total number of judges who might thus be appointed and also a limit on the potential size of any one of our Federal courts.

These proposals do not raise any issue of constitutional law. They do not suggest any form of compulsory retirement for incumbent judges. Indeed, those who have reached the retirement age, but desire to continue their judicial work, would be able to do so under less physical and mental strain and would be able to play a useful part in relieving the growing congestion in the business of our courts. Among them are men of eminence and great ability whose services the government would be loath to lose.

If, on the other hand, any judge eligible for retirement should feel that his court would suffer because of an increase in its membership, he may retire or resign under already existing provisions of law if he wishes so to do. In this connection let me say that the pending proposal to extend to the justices of the Supreme Court the same retirement privileges now available to other Federal judges, has my entire approval.

One further matter requires immediate attention. We have witnessed the spectacle of conflicting decisions in both trial and appellate courts on the constitutionality of every form of important legislation. Such a welter of uncomposed differences of judicial opinion has brought the law, the courts, and, indeed, the entire administration of justice dangerously near to disrepute.

A Federal statute is held legal by one judge in one district; it is simultaneously held illegal by another judge in another district. An act valid in one judicial circuit is invalid in another judicial circuit. Thus rights fully accorded to one group of citizens may be denied to others. As a practical matter this means that for periods running as long as one year or two years or three years — until final determination can be made by the Supreme Court — the law loses its most indispensable element — equality.

Moreover, during the long processes of preliminary motions, original trials, petitions for rehearings, appeals, reversals on technical grounds requiring re-trials, motions before the Supreme Court and the final hearing by the highest tribunal — during all this time labor, industry, agriculture, commerce and the government itself go through an unconscionable period of uncertainty and embarrassment. And it is well to remember that during these long processes the normal operations of society and government are handicapped in many cases by differing and divided opinions in the lower courts and by the lack of any clear guide for the dispatch of business. Thereby our legal system is fast losing another essential of justice — certainty.

Finally, we find the processes of government itself brought to a complete stop from time to time by injunctions issued almost automatically, sometimes even without notice to the government, and not infrequently in clear violation of the principle of equity that injunctions should be granted only in those rare cases of manifest illegality and irreparable damage against which the ordinary course of the law offers no protection. Statutes which the Congress enacts are set aside or suspended for long periods of time, even in cases to which the government is not a party.

In the uncertain state of the law, it is not difficult for the ingenious to devise novel reasons for attacking the validity of new legislation or its application. While these questions are laboriously brought to issue and debated through a series of courts, the government must stand aside. It matters not that the Congress has enacted the law, that the Executive has signed it and that the administrative machinery is waiting to function.

Government by injunction lays a heavy hand upon normal processes; and no important statute can take effect — against any individual or organization with the means to employ lawyers and engage in wide-flung litigation — until it has passed through the whole hierarchy of the courts.

Thus the judiciary, by postponing the effective date of acts of the Congress, is assuming an additional function and is coming more and more to constitute a scattered, loosely organized and slowly operating third house of the national Legislature.

This state of affairs has come upon the nation gradually over a period of decades. In my annual message to this Congress I expressed some views and some hopes.

Now, as an immediate step, I recommend that the Congress provide that no decision, injunction, judgment or decree on any constitutional question be promulgated by any Federal court without previous and ample notice to the Attorney General and an opportunity for the United States to present evidence and be heard. This is to prevent court action on the constitutionality of acts of the Congress in suits between private individuals, where the government is not a party to the suit, without giving opportunity to the Government of the United States to defend the law of the land.

I also earnestly recommend that in cases in which any court of first instance determines a question of constitutionality, the Congress provide that there shall be a direct and immediate appeal to the Supreme Court, and that such cases take precedence over all other matters pending in that court. Such legislation will, I am convinced, go far to alleviate the inequality, uncertainty and delay in the disposition of vital questions of constitutionality arising under our fundamental law.

My desire is to strengthen the administration of justice and to make it a more effective servant of public need. In the American ideal of government the courts find an essential and constitutional place. In striving to fulfill that ideal, not only the judges but the Congress and the Executive as well, must do all in their power to bring the judicial organization and personnel to the high standards of usefulness which sound and efficient government and modern conditions require.

This message has dealt with four present needs:

First, to eliminate congestion of calendars and to make the judiciary as a whole less static by the constant and systematic addition of new blood to its personnel; second, to make the judiciary more elastic by providing for temporary transfers of circuit and district judges to those places where Federal courts are most in arrears; third, to furnish the Supreme Court practical assistance in supervising the conduct of business in the lower courts; fourth, to eliminate inequality, uncertainty and delay now existing in the determination of constitutional questions involving Federal statutes.

If we increase the personnel of the Federal courts so that cases may be promptly decided in the first instance and may be given adequate and prompt hearing on all appeals; if we invigorate all the courts by the persistent infusion of new blood; if we grant to the Supreme Court further power and responsibility in maintaining the efficiency of the entire Federal judiciary, and if we assure government participation in the speedier consideration and final determination of all constitutional questions, we shall go a long way toward our high objectives. If these measures achieve their aim, we may be relieved of the necessity of considering any fundamental changes in the powers of the courts or the Constitution of our government — changes which involve consequences so far-reaching as to cause uncertainty as to the wisdom of such course.

B. THE ATTORNEY GENERAL'S LETTER

The President
The White House

My dear Mr. President:

Delay in the administration of justice is the outstanding defect of our Federal judicial system. It has been a cause of concern to practically every one of my predecessors in office. It has exasperated the bench, the bar, the business community and the public.

The litigant conceives the judge as one promoting justice through the mechanism of the courts. He assumes that the direct-ing power of the judge is exercised over its officers from the time a case is filed with the clerk of the court. He is entitled to assume that the judge is pressing forward litigation in the full recognition of the principle that "justice delayed is justice denied."

It is a mockery of justice to say to a person when he files suit that he may receive a decision years later. Under a properly ordered system rights should be determined promptly. The course of litigation should be measured in months and not in years.

Yet in some jurisdictions the delays in the administration of justice are so interminable that to institute suit is to embark on a lifelong adventure. Many persons submit to acts of injustice rather than resort to the courts. Inability to secure a prompt judicial adjudication leads to improvident and unjust settlements.

Moreover, the time factor is an open invitation to those who are disposed to institute unwarranted litigation or interpose unfounded defenses in the hope of forcing an adjustment which could not be secured upon the merits. This situation frequently results in extreme hardships. The small business man or the litigant of limited means labors under a grave and constantly increasing disadvantage because of his inability to pay the price of justice.

Statistical data indicate that in many districts a disheartening and unavoidable interval must elapse between the date that issue is joined in a pending case and the time when it can be reached for trial in due course. These computations do not take into account the delays that occur in the preliminary stages of litigation or the postponements after a case might normally be expected to be heard.

The evil is a growing one. The business of the courts is continually increasing in volume, importance, and complexity. The average case load borne by each judge has grown nearly fifty per cent since 1913, when the district courts were first organized on their present basis. When the courts are working under such pressure it is inevitable that the character of their work must suffer.

The number of new cases offset those that are disposed of, so that the courts are unable to decrease the enormous backing of undigested matters. More than fifty thousand pending cases (exclusive of bankruptcy proceedings) overhang the Federal dockets — a constant menace to the orderly processes of justice. Whenever a single case requires a protracted trial, the routine business of the court is further neglected. It is an intolerable situation and we should make shift to amend it.

Efforts have been made from time to time to alleviate some of the conditions that contribute to the slow rate of speed with which causes move through the courts. The Congress has recently conferred on the Supreme Court the authority to prescribe rules of procedure after verdict in criminal cases and the power to adopt and promulgate uniform rules of practice for civil actions at law in the district courts. It has provided terms of court in certain places at which Federal courts had not previously convened. A small number of judges have been added from time to time.

Despite these commendable accomplishments, sufficient progress has not been made. Much remains to be done in developing procedure and administration, but this alone will not meet modern needs. The problem must be approached in a more comprehensive fashion if the United States is to have a judicial system worthy of the nation.

Reason and necessity require the appointment of a sufficient number of judges to handle the business of the Federal courts. These additional judges should be of a type and age which would warrant us in believing that they would vigorously attack their dockets, rather than permit their dockets to overwhelm them.

The cost of additional personnel should not deter us. It must be borne in mind that the expense of maintaining the judicial system constitutes hardly three-tenths of one per cent of the cost of maintaining the Federal establishment.

While the estimates for the current fiscal year aggregate over $23,000,000 for the maintenance of the legislative branch of the government, and over $2,100,000,000 for the permanent agencies of the executive branch, the estimated cost of maintaining the judiciary is only about $6,500,000. An increase in the judicial personnel, which I earnestly recommend, would result in a hardly perceptible percentage of increase in the total annual budget.

This result should not be achieved, however, merely by creating new judicial positions in specific circuits or districts. The reform should be effectuated on the basis of a consistent system which would revitalize our whole judicial structure and assure the activity of judges at places where the accumulation of business is the greatest. As congestion is a varying factor and cannot be foreseen, the system should be flexible and should permit the temporary assignment of judges to points where they appear to be most needed.

The newly created personnel should constitute a mobile force, available for service in any part of the country at the assignment and direction of the Chief Justice. A functionary might well be created to be known as proctor, or by some other suitable title, to be appointed by the Supreme Court and to act under its direction, charged with the duty of continuously keeping informed as to the state of Federal judicial business throughout the United States and of assisting the Chief Justice in assigning judges to pressure areas.

I append hereto certain statistical information, which will give point to the suggestions I have made.

These suggestions are designed to carry forward the program for improving the processes of justice which we have discussed and worked upon since the beginning of your first administration.

The time has come when further legislation is essential.

To speed justice, to bring it within the reach of every citizen, to free it of unnecessary entanglements and delays, are primary obligations of our government.

Respectfully submitted,
Homer S. Cummings,
Attorney General

C. DRAFT OF THE PROPOSED LAW

Sec. 1. Be it enacted by the Senate and the House of Representatives of the United States of America in Congress assembled, that

(a) When any judge of a court of the United States, appointed to hold his office during good behavior, has heretofore or hereafter attained the age of 70 years and has held a commission or commissions as judge of any such court or courts at least ten years, continuously or otherwise, and within six months thereafter has neither resigned nor retired, the President for each such judge who has not so resigned or retired, shall nominate, and by and with the advice and consent of the Senate, shall appoint one additional judge to the court to which the former is commissioned. Provided, that no additional judge shall be appointed hereunder if the judge who is of retirement age dies, resigns or retires prior to the nomination of such additional judge.

(b) The number of judges of any court shall be permanently increased by the number appointed thereto under the provisions of subsection (a) of this section. No more than fifty judges shall be appointed thereunder, nor shall any judge be so appointed if such appointment would result in (1) more than fifteen members of the Supreme Court of the United States, (2) more than two additional members so appointed to a Circuit Court of Appeals, the Court of Claims, the United States Court of Customs and Patent Appeals, or the Customs Court, or (3) more than twice the number of judges now authorized to be appointed for any district or, in the case of judges appointed for more than one district, for any such group of districts.

(c) That the number of judges which is at least two-thirds of the number of which the Supreme Court of the United States consists, or three-fifths of the number of which the United States Court of Appeals for the District of Columbia, the Court of Claims or the United States Court of Customs, and Patent Appeals consists, shall constitute a quorum of such court.

(d) An additional judge shall not be appointed under the provisions of this section when the judge who is of retirement age is commissioned to an office as to which Congress has provided that a vacancy shall not be filled.

Sec. 2. (a) Any circuit judge hereafter appointed may be designated and assigned from time to time by the Chief Justice of the United States for service in the Circuit Court of Appeals for any circuit. Any district judge hereafter appointed may be designated and assigned from time to time by the Chief Justice of the United States for service in any district court, or, subject to the authority of the Chief Justice by the senior circuit judge of his circuit for service in any district court within the circuit.

A district judge designated and assigned to another district hereunder may hold court separately and at the same time as the district judge in such district. All designations and assignments made

hereunder shall be filed in the office of the clerk and entered on the minutes of both the court from and to which a judge is designated and assigned, and thereafter the judge so designated and assigned shall be authorized to discharge all the judicial duties (except the power of appointment to a statutory position or of permanent designation of a newspaper or depository of funds) of a judge of the court to which he is designated and assigned.

The designation and assignment of a judge shall not impair his authority to perform such judicial duties of the court to which he was commissioned as may be necessary or appropriate. The designation and assignment of any judge may be terminated at any time by order of the Chief Justice or the senior circuit judge, as the case may be.

(b) After the designation and assignment of a judge by the Chief Justice, the senior circuit judge of the circuit in which such judge is commissioned may certify to the Chief Justice any consideration which such senior circuit judge believes to make advisable that the designated judge remain in or return for service in the court to which he was commissioned. If the Chief Justice deems the reasons sufficient he shall revoke, or designate the time of termination of, such designation and assignment.

(c) In case a trial or hearing has been entered upon but has not been concluded before the expiration of the period of service of a district judge designated and assigned hereunder, the period of service shall, unless terminated under the provisions of subsection (a) of this section, be deemed to be extended until the trial or hearing has been concluded. Any designated and assigned district judge who has held court in another district than his own shall have power, notwithstanding his absence from such district and the expiration of any time limit in his designation, to decide all matters which have been submitted to him within such district, to decide motions for new trials, settle bills of exceptions, certify or authenticate narratives of testimony or perform any other act required by law or the rules to be performed in order to prepare any case so tried by him for review in an Appellate Court, and his action thereon in writing filed with the clerk of the court where the trial or hearing was had shall be as valid as if such action had been taken by him within that district and within the period of his designation.

Any designated and assigned circuit judge who has sat on another court than his own shall have power, notwithstanding the expiration of any time limit in his designation, to participate in the decision of all matters submitted to the court while he was sitting and to perform or participate in any act appropriate to the disposition or review of matters submitted while he was sitting and to perform or participate in any act appropriate to the disposition or review of matters submitted while he was sitting on such court, and his action thereon shall be as valid as if it had been taken while sitting on such court and within the period of his designation.

Sec. 3. (a) The Supreme Court shall have power to appoint a proctor. It shall be his duty: (1) to obtain and, if deemed by the court to be desirable, to publish information as to the volume, character and status of litigation in the district courts and circuit courts of appeals, and such other information as the Supreme Court may from time to time require by order, and it shall be the duty of any judge, clerk or marshal of any court of

the United States promptly to furnish such information as may be required by the proctor; (2) to investigate the need of assigning district and circuit judges to other courts and to make recommendations thereon to the Chief Justice; (3) to recommend, with the approval of the Chief Justice, to any court of the United States methods for expediting cases pending on its dockets; and (4) to perform such other duties consistent with his office as the court shall direct.

(b) The proctor shall, by requisition upon the public printer, have any necessary printing and binding done at the government printing office, and authority is conferred upon the public printer to do such printing and binding.

(c) The salary of the proctor shall be $10,000 per annum, payable out of the Treasury in monthly installments, which shall be in full compensation for the services required by law. He shall also be allowed, in the discretion of the Chief Justice, stationery, supplies, travel expenses, equipment, necessary professional and clerical assistance and miscellaneous expenses appropriate for performing the duties imposed by this section. The expenses in connection with the maintenance of his office shall be paid from the appropriation of the Supreme Court of the United States.

Sec. 4. There is hereby authorized to be appropriated, out of any money in the Treasury not otherwise appropriated, the sum of $100,000 for the salaries of additional judges and the other purposes of this act during the fiscal year 1937.

Sec. 5. When used in this act —(a) The term "judge of retirement age" means a judge of a court of the United States, appointed to hold his office during good behavior, who has attained the age of 70 years and has held a commission or commissions as judge of any such court or courts at least ten years, continuously or otherwise, and within six months thereafter, whether or not he is eligible for retirement, has neither resigned nor retired.

(b) The term "Circuit Court of Appeals" includes the United States Court of Appeals for the District of Columbia; the term "senior circuit judge" includes the Chief Justice of the United States Court of Appeals for the District of Columbia, and the term "circuit" includes the District of Columbia.

(c) The term "district court" includes the district court of the District of Columbia but does not include the district court in any territory or insular possession.

(d) The term "judge" includes justice.

Sec. 6. This act shall take effect on the thirtieth day after the date of its enactment.

EDITORIAL COMMENTS

A. THE NEW YORK HERALD-TRIBUNE

IN this one hundred and sixty-first year of the independence of the United States, President Roosevelt has brought forward a proposal which, if enacted into law, would end the American State as it has existed throughout the long years of its life.

The plan is put forward with all the artistry of the President's political mind. He speaks in the name of "youth," always a popular and appealing note. He dangles before the House and Senate fifty new and important jobs, always ripe and luscious bait for the Congressional mind. He ingeniously conveys the impression that all he seeks is a routine and moderate effort to speed up justice and improve the whole Federal bench.

Yet, beneath this veneer of politeness, the brutal fact is that President Roosevelt would pack the Supreme Court with six new justices of his own choosing.

No President of the United States ever before made the least gesture toward attempting to gain such a vast grant of power. Mr. Roosevelt demands it, calmly, artfully. By one legislative act, availing himself of the one loophole in the Constitution — the failure to specify the number of members in the Supreme Court — he would strike at the roots of that equality of the three branches of government upon which the nation is founded, and centralize in himself the control of judicial, as well as executive functions.

It was a French King, Louis XIV, who said, "L'état, c'est moi"—"I am the State." The paper shell of American constitutionalism would continue if President Roosevelt secured the passage of the law he now demands. But it would be only a shell.

Editorial, *The New York Herald-Tribune*, February 6, 1937. Used by permission.

B. THE NEW YORK TIMES
The President's Plan

Three principal arguments have been advanced in behalf of the President's plan to alter the personnel of the Supreme Court by act of Congress. First, it is said that the present court is obstructing orderly social progress by its practice of invalidating necessary measures enacted by the Administration. Second, it is claimed that in the last election the President received a virtual mandate to put an end to this situation, even though he did not propose or discuss his present method of doing it. Third, it is asserted that the President has chosen the wisest course of action available to him in the circumstances.

I

As for the first of these arguments, the argument that the court is blocking social progress, the record shows that eight laws enacted by the Roosevelt Administration have been held unconstitutional. These eight laws are:

1. A measure providing for the conversion of building and loan associations to Federal charters.
2. A measure which was never on the Administration's own program, but which was forced on it through a filibuster staged by Huey Long, providing for a moratorium on farm mortgages.
3. A measure which the President said was "crudely drawn" and which was signed by him only after "a difficult decision," providing for the payment of railway pensions.
4. An act, known as the Municipal Bankruptcy Act, of which practically no use was ever made.

5. A "hot oil" law for the petroleum industry, which dealt with a situation which is no longer present.
6. The law creating NRA, a statute held to be flagrantly unconstitutional by a unanimous Supreme Court, including its three stanch liberals, precisely at the time when Congress was preparing to discard the measure anyway.
7. AAA, which has been both defended and denounced at length, but which was in any case a pre-drought measure for the prevention of farm surpluses which do not exist at present.
8. The Guffey Coal Act, which established a "little NRA" for the bituminous coal industry, with provisions which included wages-and-hours regulations.

In addition to these eight measures, there are two others which may be held unconstitutional at the present session of the court. One is the Public Utility Act of 1935, a measure whose "death sentence clause" has been criticized by many reasonable people as high-handed and confiscatory. The other is the Wagner Labor Relations Act, an admittedly partisan measure, drawn solely in the interest of a single group and of so little practical value that the Government itself made no use of it in the case of the most important labor controversy to arise since the passage of the act.

It must be said, of course, that this list does not include the New York Minimum Wage Law, a measure held to be unconstitutional in a regrettable 5-to-4 decision handed down last June. But this decision

Editorial, *The New York Times,* "The President's Plan," February 14, 1937, section 4, page 8. Used by permission.

involved a State law, not an enactment of the Roosevelt Administration, and it is reasonable to believe that the normal process of change in the court's membership will alter its position on such State legislation at an early date. The switch of a single vote would be sufficient for this purpose.

Of the Roosevelt Administration's own program, it is fair to say that the eight measures which have been declared unconstitutional, and the two which may be held unconstitutional at the present session, are not the measures which have won the President the support of many thoughtful, middle-of-the-road progressives. Doubtless these measures have appealed to various "blocs" and factions. But it is difficult to believe that, for the nation as a whole, they really represent the best work of the Roosevelt Administration — work to be placed on a par with such statesmanlike achievements as its foreign policy, its reciprocal trade agreements, its revision of the banking laws, its reorganization of the Federal Reserve System, its regulation of the Stock Exchanges, its control of the issuance of securities, its social security legislation, its brilliant handling of the bank panic.

It is still more difficult to believe that the social progress of the country has really been obstructed by the invalidation of a particular group of eight measures, some of which were forced on the Administration against its will, some of which dealt with situations no longer in existence, some of which were seldom used, and some of which achieved in the long run the intense unpopularity and the widespread disregard which characterized the last days of NRA.

II

The President apparently having reached a different conclusion, we come to the second argument: namely, the question of his "mandate."

Those who hold that he received a mandate in the last election for his present plan do not attempt to argue that the Democratic platform embodied the proposal he now offers, or to assert that the President himself so much as mentioned this plan on a single occasion during the entire course of his campaign. Rather, they rely upon one or the other of two deductions: either they say that the country must have known that the President would change the personnel of the Supreme Court in any case, in the event of his re-election, as rapidly as its present members died, retired or resigned, or else they say that the Republicans repeatedly charged that the President would do something of the kind that he has now done, and that they thereby made the issue for him.

So far as the first theory is concerned, the President has now shown that he is unwilling to wait for the present members of the court to die, retire or resign. As for the second theory, it must be said that a mandate achieved by the process of failing to reply to the accusation of an adversary is circuitously obtained.

One thing can be said with certainty: the President has no mandate for this plan from those who would have withheld their support from him in the last election had they known during the campaign that he would subsequently pursue this course.

III

The third argument in behalf of the President's proposal is that it represents the wisest and least dangerous course of action available to him in the present circumstances. From this opinion we dissent. The wisest course for Mr. Roosevelt to follow was the course which this newspaper ventured on more than one occasion to hope that he would follow during his second Administration. This course, as it seemed clearly to be indicated both by the needs of the occasion and by the President's own apparent recognition of these needs, was to consolidate as effectively as possible the gains of the recovery movement; to perfect the many reforms and innovations already introduced, before risking new adventures; to rid the President's office of the vast, unhealthy "war powers" vested in it during the emergency of the depression, rather than to seek still further powers; to restore the normal processes of democratic government in this country, after the storm of 1929 to 1933, by decentralizing the heavily overcentralized authority of government and by strengthening once more the traditional American system of checks and balances.

That course was the wisest course for the President to pursue. It is not a course from which he was swerved by influences beyond his control. For it is difficult to believe that the present Congress could force on the President a major policy objectionable to him, by a two-thirds vote overriding a Presidential veto.

If, however, Mr. Roosevelt chose to propose a change in the Constitution or the court, a constitutional amendment giving the country an opportunity to express an opinion directly on the question would have been preferable to the plan which he has followed. There would have been certain inevitable dangers in any amendment which might have been proposed. But at least this method would have had the merit of meeting the issue squarely, without exposing the Administration to the charge that it has sought to solve a great constitutional question by resort to political cleverness.

C. THE NEW REPUBLIC
The President Faces the Court

Those who have been complaining that President Roosevelt, in announcing his proposal for the Supreme Court, did not speak the entire contents of his mind, can do so no longer. In the series of public utterances on this subject, of which the first was the speech on March 4, he has gone straight to the heart of the matter.

The Court, he says bluntly, is preventing the things that need to be done, that can only be done by the federal government and that are desired, as the election returns showed, by a large majority of the American people. He recalls the action of the Court on the AAA, the NRA, the Railroad Retirement Act, the Guffy Coal Act, and the New York Minimum Wage Law. He points to adverse decisions of the lower federal courts on the TVA and the Wagner Labor Relations Law, decisions which he clearly expects the Supreme Court to sustain. He declares that in regard to relief for the farmer, the maintenance of minimum standards for labor, control of floods and droughts and the generation of cheap power, action is needed and needed now. He disavows any intention to break with American tradition and seek a third term for himself. His ambition is

on January 20, 1941, to turn over this desk and chair in the White House to my succes-

"The President Faces the Court," *The New Republic*, LXXXX, No. 1163 (March 17, 1937), 153–154. Used by permission.

sor, whoever he may be, with the assurance that I am at the same time turning over to him, as President, a nation intact, a nation at peace, a nation prosperous, a nation clear in its knowledge of what powers it has to serve its own citizens, a nation that is in the position to use those powers to the full in order to move forward steadily to meet the modern needs of humanity — a nation which has thus proved that the democratic form and methods of national government can and will succeed.

The President, in short, has turned on the heat. In last week's issue of *The New Republic* our Washington correspondent commented on the fact that Mr. Roosevelt was permitting the Court fight to move at its own pace, that he had abstained from putting any pressure on anyone and contented himself with private discussion with members of Congress conducted in an atmosphere of gentle persuasion. In the intervening seven days, he has changed his tactics notably. He is appealing to the country in the expectation that the people will make their voices heard in Senate and House. There are already evidences that this expectation is being realized.

That the President's indictment of the Court, at last made with such vigor and frankness, is a just one, seems to us beyond dispute. It is quite true that in some of the decisions hostile to the New Deal the liberal minority participated; but it was to the devices used, and not to the end sought, that the members of the minority objected. The members of the majority have demonstrated time and time again that when there is a conflict between human rights and those of property it is to the latter that their allegiance is given. They have created, as Mr. Roosevelt pointed out last week and as *The New Republic* has often stated in the past, a no man's land in which neither

federal nor state government is able to control. They refuse to admit the necessities of a changing world, no matter how great may be the cost of their refusal in the frustration and suffering of millions of their fellow Americans.

It is quite true that the President's proposal does not completely solve the problem presented by the fact that the Court in recent decades has arrogated to itself vast powers never contemplated by the authors of the Constitution. Indeed, his suggestion is only a first step. Everyone recognized that the future course of action of additional Justices appointed by Mr. Roosevelt or any of his successors is unpredictable. There is no magic in a Court of any given size and no guarantee that a new personnel would invariably pursue a course in the best interest of all the American people. We have repeatedly pointed out in recent weeks that the President's suggestion is but a necessary first step, a breaking of the immediate deadlock by the only device, so far as we are aware, that anyone has suggested that is both constitutional and capable of being put into effect within a reasonably brief period of time. Additional action is also needed and undoubtedly this additional action includes a constitutional amendment. It will in all probability take many years to deflate the Court and restore it to its proper relationship to other government branches.

It is now clear, in our opinion, that neither the President nor anyone else has any marked enthusiasm for the device now under consideration. But no one has any enthusiasm, either, for the situation into which the conservative majority of the Court has brought us by a series of political decisions, politically inspired. Those who are now protesting with hysterical vehemence against a "presidential dictatorship" were silent over many years about a far more serious Court dictatorship, one that carried a deeper threat to American institutions than anything President Roosevelt has done or tried to do. The chief valid criticism of Mr. Roosevelt is not that he is now seeking to mitigate that dictatorship but that for so long a period of time he should have passively accepted its consequences.

D. THE NATION
Purging the Supreme Court

There can be little doubt that Mr. Roosevelt's attack on government by senility has been a brilliant tour de force. The right is dismayed by it. The left is confused. The country as a whole is puzzled and entertained. No wonder the President felt a bit prankish when he read the message at his press conference. But the question of the adequacy of the proposal remains. Our answer will probably remind the reader of the Scottish jury that came back with the verdict, "Not guilty, but don't do it again." We by no means feel that the President has chosen the best plan — but along with a better plan it deserves support. The proposal is in the form of a reorganization of the federal judiciary. It finds the cause of the delays in justice in the failure of judges to retire at seventy. It proposes that for each judge who refused thus to retire an additional judge shall be appointed to his court, provided that the size of the Supreme Court shall not exceed fifteen. There is every indication that the President is giving the Supreme Court judges a dose of their own medicine — legalism. He adopts the Supreme Court's method of disguising important changes in state policy behind a screen of innocent-seeming legality. It is unjust to accuse the President of duplicity. He is doing exactly what Justice Roberts did when he talked elaborately of states' rights and killed the processing taxes. Two can play at that game, and in the realm of high strategy the Supreme Court has met its master.

But it is not all play. What the President is proposing is to dynamite the reactionary judges into retirement. To effect this he uses the most convenient handle — old age. But it is a handle to a very real grievance, in the lower federal courts as well as in the Supreme Court. There are four sitting members of the Third Circuit Court of Appeals. Their average age is seventy-seven and one-half years. It is Judge Buffington of this court, over eighty-one, who has been holding up the Pennsylvania Greyhound case, involving the Wagner Labor Act, since 1935. With respect to the Supreme Court, the Roosevelt luck, it must be remembered, has not operated. No appointments have fallen to him. He has had to sit by helplessly and watch the years accumulate and men decay. He now presents the tory judges with the bitterest hemlock cup any tory has had to quaff. Six of the present court are over seventy, only one of them — Brandeis — definitely a liberal. If they genuinely wish to keep the court from being "packed," they can hold the number down to nine by retiring. Whichever

"Purging the Supreme Court," *The Nation*, CXLIV, No. 7 (February 13, 1937), 173–174. Used by permission.

ones do not choose to retire must bear the responsibility of permanently increasing the court's number by that many.

One thing is clear. Mr. Roosevelt has been at least consistent. He has since the NRA decision steadily held that the Constitution needs no change if it is interpreted liberally. He has deftly sidestepped the three plans that have been most vigorously pushed — giving Congress the power to override the Supreme Court's veto, limiting the Supreme Court veto to at least a two-thirds' vote, giving Congress explicit power (by amendment) to regulate industry and agriculture. He has evidently considered that these measures would be at once too radical, since they would directly curb the judicial power or reestablish the supremacy of Congress, and also too dilatory, since each one might — by raising questions of constitutionality — have to be enacted finally as an amendment. His present plan does not touch the judicial power, and does not change the relation of the court to Congress. There can be no question of its constitutionality. It neither seeks to curb the court nor (despite the current impression) pack it, for if the judges retire there is no increase in numbers. Rather it purges the court by removing the infirm, and therefore (by a rough and imperfect logic) the least fit.

Where the President got the plan and why he should have sprung it just now are not entirely clear. Paul Ward points out in the *Baltimore Sun* that a similar technique was proposed in an 1869 bill in Grant's Administration, but failed of passage. The theory that he may have wished to influence favorably the Wagner Act cases seems untenable; if anything the proposal is calculated to freeze the judges into sheer immobility through rage. There may be some relation to the automobile strike and the power jam, as warnings to the business community that the President has trump cards which he is willing to play. But our own guess — and it is only a guess — is that Mr. Roosevelt wished to seize the occasion when public sentiment was ripe for action of some sort but before the movements for more radical curbs on the court had grown too strong to be stopped.

There are basic objections to the President's plan. It clearly does not meet the issue of the judicial power as an obstruction to democratic action. It does not go to the root of our judicial oligarchy, but by reorganizing it seeks rather to perpetuate it. There is a danger that, especially after the number of fifteen has been reached, a justice will wait until he has a favorable President before resigning, thus creating a semi-hereditary caste. It can be used as effectively by a reactionary President as by a liberal, and ultimately it may produce simply a benchful of younger reactionaries — just as blind and stubborn in their fifties as in their seventies. Moreover, even a liberal President finds that there's many a slip between the nomination of a judge and his decisions: be it eternally remembered that McReynolds was appointed by Wilson. And certainly Mr. Roosevelt, judging from the names most mooted now, cannot be depended upon to choose more wisely than his predecessors.

Nevertheless, it is the task of progressives to support the measure — with an open-eyed awareness of its shortcomings. It will clear the blockage of New Deal legislation — at least for the immediate future. Meanwhile it will have delivered a blow to the sanctity of the Supreme Court from which the court will never wholly recover. If the court can be defeated once, it can be defeated again —

and that is a lesson from which the people will profit. While logically the plan is leaky, psychologically it is sound. For talk as we may about educating the common man on the judicial power, the thing that sticks in his mind is that the men who exercise it are old men and therefore probably behind the times.

But for progressives to support this measure does not mean that they should stop there. *Purging the Supreme Court does not preclude curbing it.* A movement for a constitutional amendment must be launched now, so that when the rejuvenated court again grows ossified, we shall not have to fight the same battle all over again. But to refuse support to Mr. Roosevelt's measure and to hold out for "an amendment or nothing" is now — whatever it may have been before — playing into the hands of the reactionaries. They will inveigh against "packing" the court, grow hysterical about the supposed blow to the independence of the judiciary, and insist that the only method of change is through an amendment. Do not be trapped by them. The only thing they value in an amendment is the delay it would involve and their hope finally of being able to beat it. And without Roosevelt's support for an amendment, that hope would be a reality. With his support it is possible to push on the campaign for constitutional reform, viewing the present proposal merely as the opening gun in a battle

that will be protracted and fiercely disputed. In such a battle what the progressives have chiefly to overcome is the myth of Supreme Court divinity. When they have conquered that, they can move on to achieve democracy.

Our program is, then, for progressives to support Roosevelt's proposal if he will support them in simultaneously launching an amendment. In that spirit we present, . . . our candidates for the six new posts. We have omitted members of the present Congress, since they would be barred until the end of their term from occupying posts they had themselves created. This has made it necessary to exclude several excellent choices. We submit the list with the earnest reminder that what value there is in the plan will be completely sacrificed unless genuine liberals are chosen.

The Nation's CANDIDATES

1. Professor Felix Frankfurter — Harvard Law School.
2. Dean Lloyd Garrison — Wisconsin Law School.
3. Chairman J. Warren Madden — National Labor Relations Board.
4. Professor Walton H. Hamilton — Yale Law School and Social Security Board.
5. Robert H. Jackson — Assistant Attorney General.
6. Herman Oliphant — General Counsel U. S. Treasury.

Bernard DeVoto:

DESERTION FROM THE NEW DEAL

ON the day after the Senate killed the Supreme Court bill the Easy Chair went round to see Eli Potter. Eli was the one political commentator who, on its announcement, had declared that the bill would be killed and who had stuck to that prediction through all the whoops and screams of the ensuing months. Furthermore, there was a rumor that Eli had resigned from the New Deal and that, if true, was news. Eli was practically the only intellectual in America not employed by the New Deal who had not already departed either to the right or to the left. He had clung firmly to the baggage-car roof with his ears full of cinders, and if he had now got off the train the Easy Chair wanted to know why.

Eli parried our question with another one. What, he said, is a communist? A communist is an American who thinks they have communism in Russia. You have observed the tempests and whirlpools set up in the communist psyche by the events of the past year in Russia, and you have noticed that the conflict thus generated has begun to make our leftist brethren ask one another a question that none of them like. Why, they are driven to ask, why do revolutions always end in Thermidor? The events of the past eight months in the United States will soon be impelling the Arthur Brisbane strain of our native stock to ask an equally uncomfortable question. Why, they will soon want to know, why do humanitarian Administrations always end in suicide?

That seemed an evasion and we repeated our question. Eli answered that he had got off the train and that he imagined a lot of other people had unloaded at about the same time. But that, he said, wasn't the important thing. The important thing was that, for the time being anyway, there was no other train for them to get aboard. The Administration had a Congress that had slipped its lead and a reaction coming which it might have cushioned, partly averted, and partly defeated if its social planning had been willing to begin with the here and now instead of concentrating on the Kingdom of God. The country was plunged into the most dangerous situation its political system can encounter, an impaired leadership midway through the second term, plus a discredited Administration with a deficit. And people like Eli, people who wanted to do what was possible to adjust the social system to the developing necessities of the modern world, would have to mark time for two, six, ten years.

We already face our worst licking since Roosevelt the First lost his nerve in 1904, Eli said, and it will be a lot worse before it's over. Roosevelt II has all but disembowelled us. While there's life there's always political adrenalin, but at the moment it looks hopeless. What are we to do? Turn Republican? Join the literary feebs in expecting the nation to pull off a communist revolution on or before Thanksgiving Day, when the greatest

Bernard DeVoto, "Desertion from the New Deal," *Harper's,* CLXXV (October, 1937), 557–560. Used by permission.

hope of the practicing communists is that they may be able within fifty years to join together the farmers and the laborers whom God has forever put asunder? Or maybe link arms with Jack Garner?

No President ever learns anything during his second term . . . all right, Eli said; you name one who did. What President Roosevelt ought to have learned from the Supreme Court fight is that neither he nor the kitchen cabinet's logic can buck a living sentiment. The national sentiment which favors separation of powers and an independent judiciary may be divinely inspired or it may be just so much Piltdown rubbish left over to clutter the great dawn of the Corcoran era, but there it is. It may be right or it may be wrong or it may have nothing to do with rightness or wrongness, but there it is. The fact was that the remodeled judiciary was not going to be independent and so the sentiment knocked it cold. And when the bill was killed, the President's second Administration was killed too, for second terms aren't educable.

The President ought also to have learned that the nation doesn't like government by ruse. Up to a point the bleachers will applaud political slickness, but the moment that point is passed they always start throwing pop bottles. If he had remembered what happened to the master ruse-makers of Congress in 1910 he might not have tried to reform the Court with hot dice. Unquestionably the country was willing to inform the Court by any means within the framework of our system that this is the twentieth century. If Mr. Roosevelt had been content to try what was possible he could have got more than he needed. But he made a blithe cast for the impossible and got nothing. Someone should have told the kitchen cabinet what happens when a jury gets a notion that the railroad lawyer is being too smart.

What an educable kitchen cabinet would have learned, Eli said, is that living sentiments still exist in this outworn republic which, they have persuaded the boss, is now going down for the third time. Maybe it is; maybe the republic had developed Cheyne-Stokes breathing. But it had sound enough reflexes left to torpedo the Supreme Court bill. It may be dying but it has more life than the kitchen cabinet's Thoroughly Rational State, and its survival makes a lot better bet than their blueprints and syllogisms.

Here Eli reminded us of what he had said when the Supreme Court bill was announced: that it was worse than a crime, sire; it was a blunder. He had opposed the bill not because he thought it could be passed but because the mere proposal was certain to endanger the Administration's whole program. But he had stayed aboard the train until it appeared that the whole program was changed — till those glittering bits of happy-dust improvisation, the government reorganization bills, came along. They proved what the Supreme Court bill had intimated: that the first Roosevelt Administration had been abandoned, that the President now thought he could do the impossible, and that he wasn't concerned about what happens when you try to do the impossible and fail.

Those bills won't pass, Eli said, so don't run a temperature. They will be killed outright or they will be amended till what began with blueprints for a new Parthenon will end in an extension to the henhouse for which the carpenter hardly needs a diagram. But the state of mind they reveal is terrifying.

For one thing they terrify those of us who think that something, not much but something, can be done with social planning. Some of what the Administration has tried looked pretty good, notably TVA, which had a good many years of work done on it by experts before the kitchen police took hold. More of it looked like the phantasies a man might entertain himself with on a train ride when he didn't have a magazine — let us not forget that the Administration proposed to end droughts forever by growing a transcontinental belt of trees where almighty God had failed to grow them. But now we get the real thing, the matured vision of the rational minds, and social planning turns out to be a set of sketches made between the soup and the entree on the back of an old envelope.

Sketches made, furthermore, by someone who had had enough cocktails to feel reckless and indifferent. Improvisations, bravura extemporizations in dynamite. Well, you can't improvise a national government and, though our liberal editors believe otherwise, you can't improvise a revolution either. The net effect is to discredit planning, and the Administration would have done better to postpone the Wholly Rational State and make some plans about the fiscal year. But it never strains at gnats, though a President named Roosevelt once told us that what hamstrings liberal governments is ignoring the fiscal year. . . .

Charles Warren:

THE SUPREME COURT IN UNITED STATES HISTORY

THAT the Court, in its one hundred and thirty years' existence, has fully and worthily fulfilled the purposes for which it was designed by the framers of the Constitution, there can be no doubt; and De Tocqueville's words, written in 1835, are as true today as then: "The Supreme Court is placed at the head of all known tribunals, both by the nature of its rights and the class of justiciable parties which it controls. The peace, the prosperity and the very existence of the Union are placed in the hands of the Judges. Without their active cooperation, the

Constitution would be a dead letter; the Executive appeals to them for protection against the encroachment of the Legislative power; the Legislature demands their protection against the designs of the Executive; they defend the Union against the disobedience of the States; the States, from the exaggerated claims of the Union; the public interests against the interests of private citizens; and the conservative spirit of order against the innovations of an excited democracy." And as Judge Field wrote, on his resignation in 1897: "As I look back over the

From *The Supreme Court in United States History* by Charles Warren, Volume II, pages 753–756. By permission of Little, Brown and Company. This statement is a summary and conclusion to Mr. Warren's review of the entire history of the Supreme Court to 1918.

more than a third of a century that I have sat on this Bench, I am more and more impressed with the immeasurable importance of this Court. Now and then we hear it spoken of as an aristocratic feature of a republican government. But it is the most democratic of all. Senators represent their States, and Representatives their constituents; but this Court stands for the whole country, and as such it is truly 'of the people, by the people and for the people.' It has, indeed, no power to legislate. It cannot appropriate a dollar of money. It carries neither the purse nor the sword. But it possesses the power of declaring the law, and in that is found the safeguard which keeps the whole mighty fabric of government from rushing to destruction. This negative power, the power of resistance, is the only safety of a popular government."

That the Court is not infallible, that like all other human institutions it makes its mistakes may be acknowledged; yet in spite of the few instances in which it has run counter to the deliberate and better judgment of the community, the American people will unquestionably conclude that final judgment as to their constitutional rights is safer in the hands of the Judiciary than in those of the Legislature, and that if either body is to possess uncontrolled omnipotence, it should be reposed in the Court rather than in Congress, and in independent Judges rather than in Judges dependent on election by the people in passionate party campaigns and on partisan political issues. In the words of Attorney-General Wickersham: "Mistakes have been made by the Judiciary. Cases have been wrongly decided and the extension of legal principles to meet new conditions and judicial interpretation of the Constitution has often been slower than impatient reformers desirous of immediate re-

sults would wish. Yet no candid critic can say that on the whole the history of the American Judiciary does not furnish as high, if not higher, example of adequate results than that of any other branch of the Government." "They have no patronage with which to reward their followers, and no partisans to sustain them right or wrong; they have no interest except in common with their countrymen, and no ambition except to leave behind them an honored name. Of all men in this world, they have the least temptation to do wrong and the greatest incentive to do right. They are not infallible, and they make their mistakes, but they make fewer mistakes than other men; and so long as they can guard the Constitution of this Republic, it will protect the lives, the liberty and the property of the American people."

This book may well close with the eloquent appeal, written in 1856 at a time when American institutions seemed shaken: "Admit that the Federal Judiciary may in its time have been guilty of errors, that it has occasionally sought to wield more power than was safe, that it is as fallible as every other human institution. Yet it has been and is, a vast agency for good; it has averted many a storm which threatened our peace, and has lent its powerful aid in uniting us together in the bonds of law and justice. Its very existence has proved a beacon of safety . . . and now let us ask ourselves, with all its imagined faults, what is there that can replace it? Strip it of its power, and what shall we get in exchange? Discord and confusion, statutes without obedience, Courts without authority, an anarchy of principles and a chaos of decision, till all law at last shall be extinguished by an appeal to arms." "If the Judiciary be struck from the system," said William Wirt in 1832, "what is there of any value that will remain? The Government cannot subsist without it. It would be as rational to talk of a solar system without a sun. No, sir, the people of the United States know the value of this institution too well to suffer it to be put down or trammelled in its action by the dictates of others."

Max Lerner:

THE SUPREME COURT AND AMERICAN CAPITALISM

THE American state has developed two of its institutions to a degree never before attained — the capitalist form of business enterprise and the judicial power. At first sight the combination seems paradoxical, joining in a single pattern an exploitative type of economic behavior with the objectivity of the judicial process. But those who have studied the building of the American state know that the paradox lies only on the surface. It is no historical accident but a matter of cultural logic that a Field should grow where a Morgan does; and a Brandeis is none the less organic a product of capitalist society than is a Debs. If the contrast between the first pair and the second is precipitous, it is none the less contrast and not contradiction. Between our business enterprise and our judicial power there is the unity of an aggressive and cohesive cultural pattern. They seem of the same fiber; have, both of them, the same toughness, richness, extravagant growth; hold out at once portent and promise.

Capitalist business enterprise, while it has reached its most consummate form in the United States, is generic to the whole Western world. But the judicial power — or more exactly, judicial supremacy — is a uniquely American institution: it could arise only in a federal state which attempts, as we do, to drive a wedge of constitutional uniformity through heterogeneous sectional and economic groupings. The core of judicial supremacy is of course the power of judicial review of legislative acts and administrative decisions. And the exercise of that power by the United States Supreme Court has made it not only "the world's most powerful court" but the focal point of our bitterest political and constitutional polemics.

At the heart of these polemics is the recognition that the real meaning of the Court is to be found in the political rather than the legal realm, and that its concern is more significantly with power politics than with judicial technology. The Court itself of course, in its official theory of its own function, disclaims any relation to the province of government or the formation of public policy; it pictures itself as going about quietly applying permanent canons of interpretation to the settlement of individual disputes. If there is any truth in this position the Court's quietness must be regarded as that of the quiet spot in the center of a tornado. However serene it may be or may pretend to be in itself, the Court is the focal point of a set of dynamic forces which play havoc with the landmarks of the American state and determine the power of configuration of the day. Whatever may be true of the function of private law as restricting itself to the settlement of disputes and the channeling of conduct in society, public law in a constitutional state operates to shift or stabilize the balance of social power.

There has been a tendency in some quarters to regard the power function of the Court as the result of an imperialistic expansion by which the justices have pushed their way to a "place in the sun." We still think in the shadow of Montesquieu and view the political process as an equation in governmental powers. The growth of the Court's power has, by this conception, taken place at the expense of the legislative and executive departments, and the American state has become the slave of a judicial oligarchy. The literature in which this enslavement is traced and expounded is voluminous, polemical, and, even when very able, somewhat dull. It is dull with the dullness of a thin and mechanical *leitmotiv* — the theory of usurpation, of the deliberate annexation by the Court of powers never intended for it. This theory is part of the general philosophy of political equilibrium which, originating with the eighteenth-century *philosophes,* was reinforced by nineteenth-century physics. It holds that the safety of the individual can be assured only by maintaining a balance between the departments of the state. Whatever may have been the valid-

ity of such a philosophy in a pre-industrial age, it has become archaic in a period when government is itself dwarfed by the new economic forces. It is as if generals in a besieged city should quarrel over precedence while the enemy was thundering at the gates.

There was, let it be admitted, a period in which the problem of judicial usurpation was a lively issue. Readers of Beveridge's volumes on Marshall are struck by the bitter political tone of the early years of the Court, beginning even with its decision in *Chisholm v. Georgia.* Charge and countercharge, invective and recrimination were staple, and in the din of party conflict it was no wonder that the still small voice of judicial objectivity was often completely drowned. In such an atmosphere usurpation had meaning and utility. The polity was in its formative stage, and there was little about the constitutional structure that was irrevocably settled. The Revolution had hewn out a new world but, as we who have been contemporaries of another Revolution can well understand, the task of giving that world content and precision of outline still remained. In the jockeying for political position and the general scramble for advantage, every argument counted, and much of the political theory of the day can be best understood in terms of this orientation toward the distribution of power. But what counted even more than theory was the *fait accompli.* Every new governmental step was decisive for later power configurations, and might some day be used as precedent. And the battles of the giants, Marshall's battles with Jefferson and Jackson, were the battles of men who knew how to use the *fait accompli.*

The Court has then from the very beginning been part of the power structure of the state, acting as an interested arbiter of disputes between the branches of the government and between the states and the federal government, and with an increasingly magistral air distributing the governmental powers. But to a great extent the significant social struggles of the first half-century of the new state were waged outside the Court. Each period has its characteristic clashes of interests and its characteristic battlegrounds where those clashes occur. In the pre-industrial period the party formations measured with a rough adequacy the vital sectional, economic, and class differences in the country. The party battles of the period had some meaning, and accumulated stresses could find release through changes of party power. The function of the Supreme Court in this scheme lay rather in settling the lines of the polity than in resolving disputes that could not be resolved outside. But when party formations grew increasingly blurred and issues such as slavery and industrialism arose to cut across party lines, an attempt was made, notably in the Dred Scott case, to draw the Supreme Court into the struggle over social policy. The attempt was of course disastrous, for the slavery issue reached too deep to the economic and emotional foundations of the life of the day to be resolved by a counting of heads of more or less partisan judges. It is significant that the most direct effect of the Dred Scott decision was the sudden growth to power of a new political party, which should settle the basic question of public policy in the approved manner at the polls. The subsequent resort to war revealed that there might be some issues so basic that they could not be settled at all within the constitutional framework.

The coming of industrialism cut clear across the orientation and function of the Court as it cut across every other phase of American life. The doctrine of judicial review, whatever may have been its precedents and whatever the legalisms of its growth, had become by the middle of the century an integral part of the American political system. But it was not the dominant political institution, nor had it acquired the compelling incidence upon public policy that it has today. Before that could happen there had to be such a shift in the nature of the state that the characteristic clashes of interest would be taken out of the sphere of democratic control. In short, only through the building of an extra-democratic structure of reality upon the framework of a democratic theory could the judicial power be given a real vitality or the Supreme Court attain its present towering command over the decision of public policy.

That transformation was effected by the maturing of capitalism with its strange combination of individualism as a pattern of belief and the corporation as a pattern of control. Business enterprise furnished the setting within which the Court was to operate, and in this setting the ramifications of the problems that came up for solution effected a complete change in the meaning and function of the judicial power. That power had always, when exercised, had far-reaching effects upon the process of our national life; even when in abeyance it had been a force to be reckoned with. The Court by expounding and applying the written Constitution had always itself been one of the elements that determined the shape and direction of the real constitution — the operative controls of our society. But the real constitution became under capitalism merely the *modus operandi* of business enterprise. Between it on the one hand, and on the other the ideals of the American experiment and the phrases in which the eighteenth century had clothed those ideals, there was an ever-lengthening gulf: it became the function of the Supreme Court to bridge that gulf. Capitalist enterprise in America generated, as capitalism has everywhere generated, forces in government and in the underlying classes hostile to capitalistic expansion and bent upon curbing it: it became the function of the Court to check those forces and to lay down the lines of economic orthodoxy. For the effective performance of its purposes capitalist enterprise requires legal certainty amidst the flux of modern life, legal uniformity amidst the heterogeneous conditions and opinions of a vast sprawling country, the legal vesting of interests amidst the swift changes of a technological society: to furnish it with these was the huge task which the Supreme Court had successfully to perform. The Court had of course other functions, and may be regarded from other angles. But if we seek a single and consistent body of principles which will furnish the rationale of the judicial power in the past half-century, we must find in it the dynamics of American business enterprise.

The steady growth in the judicial power and the increasing evidences of its economic affiliations have made the Court one of the great American ogres, part of the demonology of liberal and radical thought. It has served, in fact, as something of a testing-ground for political attitudes of every complexion. The Marxist, making the whole of politics merely an addendum to capitalism, sees the Court as the tool and capitalism as the primary force. The contemporary Jeffersonian, fearful of all centralizing power and zealous for the liberties of the common man, fears Wall Street and the Supreme Court alternately, uncertain as to which is the shadow and which the substance. His cousin the liberal, if he is of a constructive turn, counts on using the machinery of the Court to control in a statesmanlike fashion a developing capitalism which it is futile to turn back; or, if he has lost faith in the efficacy of tinkering with governmental machinery and has become an ethical liberal, he refuses to regard either Big Business or the Supreme Court in itself important, but looks to the quality of the American experience that flows through them both. The technological liberal, who thinks in blueprints and plans for state planning, regards the Court as the great technical obstruction that his plans must meet, and racks his brain for ingenious ways of avoiding the encounter.

The contemporary indictment of the Court, which furnishes the point of departure for all these shades of opinion, is in the large well known. It holds that the Court's decisions can be better explained by economic bias than by judicial objectivity, and that its trend has been to bolster the *status quo*. This indictment is itself of course far from objective. It is the expression of an attitude. And that attitude can be best studied in relation to its genesis in the Progressive movement, which ran its brief course between the turn of the twentieth century and the American entrance into the war. To that movement may be traced the current "economic interpretation" of the Court, which links its decisions with the growth of capitalism. The Marxists might of course claim this approach as deriving from their own "materialist" conception, diluted or vulgarized in the course of its transmission to our shores. But whatever the degree of logical identity with Marxist materialism, in its actual historical growth the economic interpretation of the Supreme Court is a native product. It was out of the characteristic social conflicts of the Progressive period that the economic approach to the Court emerged, and from the intellectual dilemmas of the period that it received its formulation. In fact, if one still detects in the attitude of liberal critics of the Court an equivocal and confused note, it may be found not wholly alien to the irresoluteness, the divided sense of hostility and acceptance that lay at the heart of the Progressive movement. . . .

It is obvious that the large movements of modern law can be understood best in relation to this development of a capitalist society. The ways of life and the property attitudes of this society while it was still rural and bourgeois have written themselves into the Anglo-American common law. They have written themselves also into American constitutional law, as embodied first in the written document drawn up by a group of "men of substance" acting as spokesmen for the more or less property-conscious American society of the late eighteenth century, and as interpreted by a property-conscious Supreme Court. In all societies the historical function of law has been to elaborate, rationalize, and protect the dominant institutions and the accredited ways of life, and the function of public law has been to apply ultimately the coercion of the state toward maintaining the outlines of those dominant institutions. American constitutional law, whatever may be its unique modes of operation and principles of growth, is not exempt from this function.

But here as everywhere the large historical generalization conceals great dangers. To say that American constitutional law rationalizes and gives sanction to American capitalist society is of little value unless the relation between the two is traced historically and with an eye to the evolving character of each. As with

all words that have grown to be symbols and are moved about as counters in argument, capitalism has taken on for us a singleness of meaning that beclouds more issues than it illumines. Actually of course it is not only an exceedingly complex institution, reaching out into many domains of what men do and how they think, but it is also a rapidly shifting one. Its tremendous importance for the Supreme Court flows from this fact of its change. For to a static capitalism, however baleful or beneficent, the Court and the nation could eventually work out a harmonious adjustment, balancing somehow the demands of constitutional rules with the interests of constituent groups. But a changing capitalism is continually undoing what is done even before it has been entirely done. Being a growing thing it creates conflicts of interest, problems of control, disorders in the "economic order" while the ink is scarce dry on the statute or decision which attempted to heal the ravages of some previous change. Its superior mobility over previous systems of economic organization, such as the feudal or slave systems, derives from the fact that it rests on a rapidly moving technological base and appeals to the free and even reckless flow of individual energy. We have as a consequence the characteristic transitionalism of modern Western society and that instability of institutional arrangements which gives it its vitality. And in the United States the pace of capitalist development has been extraordinarily rapid, abbreviating the earlier stages upon which the European societies lingered for centuries, and setting the pace for the entire world in the latest stages.

The history of American capitalist development falls roughly into four periods. With due awareness of the danger of schematism, and with an eye especially to their impact upon the problem of legal control, the periods may be described as (1) pre-industrial capitalism, (2) industrial capitalism, (3) monopoly capitalism, and (4) finance capitalism. . . .

These successive shifts of focus in American economic reality have done much to determine the large sweep of American constitutional law. They have done so in a threefold way: by setting the characteristic problems that have appeared for decision before the Supreme Court, by creating the conflicts and the clashes of interests which have given those problems importance for the community, and by fashioning the ideologies which have to a large degree influenced the decisions. Put in another way the impact of American capitalistic development on the Court has been at once to pose the problems and to condition the answers.

The increasing push and thrust of economic problems upon the business of the Supreme Court has been noted by Professors Frankfurter and Landis. Within this larger trend it is interesting to analyze by what dynamics of the economic process the varied range of problems is brought into the area of decision. The ordinary groupings around legal subject matter, or the groupings around clauses in the Constitution or around devices in the Court procedure, are not entirely revealing. To know that a case is an injunction case, or that it came under a writ of certiorari, or that it appealed to the due process clause of the Fourteenth Amendment, conveys little of the context of emotion and belief that might give it meaning. The groupings might more realistically be built around those clashes of interests within the economic system or clashes of attitude about it out of which the cases proceed.

These clashes of interest are as varied of course as the economic life that they mirror. They are at once evidences of maladjustment and challenges to control. Some are concerned with the organizational aspects of capitalism, others with the incidence of its functioning, still others with the distribution of its flow of income. Thus one may find clashes of interest between workers and employers over wages or hours or working conditions or plans for social insurance; between groups of businessmen over trade practices (in the sphere of business *mores*) or the maintenance of competition (in the sphere of economic ideology); between consumers and public-utility groups over rates and services; between consumers and other business groups over prices and standards; between ownership and control groups within the corporate structure over the division of profits; between agricultural and industrial groups, Big Business and Little Business groups, groups being taxed and the government as taxer; between all sorts of groups who would stand to gain from a particular government policy, such as a grant of direct relief or an issue of legal-tender paper, and those who would stand to lose; between the interests of autonomous business control and those of state-enforced competitive enterprise; between the interests of individual enterprise and those of collective control; between those who have a property interest in the *status quo* and those who have a humanistic interest in changing it.

In short, capitalism pushes ultimately before the Court the clashes of interest that are attendant on the growth of any economic system, with the displacement in each successive phase of elements that had been useful in previous phases, with the antagonisms it generates among those who are bearing its burdens and the rivalry among those who are dividing its spoils, and with the inherent contradictions that it may possess. If it be added to this that modern capitalism is perhaps the least organic system of economic organization the world has seen —"often, though not always, a mere congeries of possessors and pursuers," J. M. Keynes has called it — and that the American social and political structure within which it operates is perhaps more sprawling and heterogeneous than that of any other major capitalist society, some notion may be had of the confusion of interests and purposes out of which it is the task of the Court to bring certainty and uniformity.

The dimensions of the task must, however, be qualified in several respects. Not every case that comes before the Court involves grave conflicts of interest or broad issues of public policy; it is only the exceptional cases that do. Moreover, the pressures and interests summarily analyzed above apply to the entire governmental process in a capitalist state, and not merely to the Court. In fact, the Court does not fight on the front lines but must be considered a reserve force. The brunt of the attack and the task of reconciling the conflicts is met by the legislatures and the administrative agencies, which are more amenable to democratic control than is a small tribunal holding office for life. It is only what survives the legislative barriers and also the jurisdictional exclusions of the Court, that comes finally to pose its issues. And even of this group not every case involving an important conflict of interests will exact from the Court that intense absorption with its social values and implications which creates the nexus binding the judicial process to the economic system. Many a case

which, if it had come later or earlier in the country's development, might have been decided differently or constituted a leading case fails at the time to call into play the entire concentration of the Court's social philosophy. For at any period neither the Court nor the country can focus its energies on more than a few dominant issues. It is the area that includes these issues — let us call it the "area of vital conflict"— that determines the path of growth in the judicial process and fashions the outlines of constitutional law. . . .

The Fourteenth Amendment, which has laid its hand so heavily upon American constitutional law, seems to have come into being with less attendant innocence than had until recently been believed. Professor Kendrick's edition of the journal of the committee which prepared the amendment indicates that the notion of using a Negro rights amendment to restrict state-legislative raids upon business interests was not wholly absent from the minds of the members. It did not receive definite expression before the Court, however, until Roscoe Conkling's argument in the San Mateo case. But even clearer was the intent on the part of the radical Republicans to use the amendment as an entering wedge to effect a complete constitutional subordination of the states to the nation, not so much in the interests of property as in the interests of northern control. The first test of the amendment in the Slaughterhouse case was therefore not a clear-cut decision on the economic issue of regulation that was involved but was oriented toward the political issue, which was more directly in the area of vital conflict of the day. But the most important parts of the decision are the brief of ex-Justice Campbell and Justice

Field's dissenting opinion that was based on it. Campbell's line of reasoning, by which the due process clause could be interpreted to support property rights against legislative restriction, was subsequently hammered away at the Court in a series of powerful dissenting opinions by Field and his supporters until their triumph in *Allgeyer v. Louisiana*. Whatever the orientation of the majority in the case, the Field orientation was economic. It is as if he had a prevision of the future needs of capitalist enterprise and how those needs would be supplied. The second and more crucial test of the Fourteenth Amendment, in *Munn v. Illinois*, was, because of its setting in the Granger revolt rather than the Reconstruction issue, fought on new ground. The impact of the monopolistic trends upon the farmers, whose position in a capitalist society is at best anachronistic, had led to the passage of regulatory state legislation. The reaction of the business community to the Waite opinion, with its attitude of judicial toleration of the state acts, and Justice Field's dissent as the expression of that reaction, marked the beginning of a *grande peur* which seized the property interests and scarcely abated for several decades until they had arrived within the secure confines of *Allgeyer v. Louisiana* and *Lochner v. New York*. It was scarcely a coincidence that this epidemic of fear coincided with the publication of Cooley's *Constitutional Limitations*. But the most significant phase of the campaign for a new conception of due process lay in the steady insistence of the counsel for the corporations that the justices owed a duty to the society they lived in to conserve its most sacred institution even in the face of the strict constitutional logic of the situation. This was the first important manifestation of the social animus of the new corporation

lawyers and of the effects of their association with the ideology of business.

This period in the Court's history from the Civil War to the first victory of the Field cohorts in the mid-eighties was thus one of the fateful periods in our national life. It marked a parting of the ways between a policy of judicial tolerance and one of the further extension of judicial review. The Court stood poised between the agrarian revolt, which had been stirred by the growth of monopoly capitalism, and the business interests, whose new militancy concealed their uneasiness. We know of course which policy eventually prevailed and what a difference that has made in our national life. It is relatively easy from the vantage-ground of the present to say that a real choice never existed, and that the development of monopoly capitalism made the outcome for the Supreme Court an inevitable one. But inevitability is a summary word that solves too many difficulties. Capitalist development certainly weighted the scales. It set the wider limits outside of which no choice was possible. But within those limits the country had a chance at a choice — and took it.

The doctrine which came to the fore in the mid-eighties and dominated the Court for a quarter-century was on the economic side a militant expression of *laissez-faire* and on the legal side a no less militant extension of the economic scope of due process. It seems at first sight surprising that a period which was seeing the individualistic ideal of competition give way to monopoly should call for a *laissez-faire* policy in its Court decisions. But *laissez-faire* is to be distinguished from individualism; the latter is a philosophy, the former a mandate. *Laissez-faire* may conceivably proceed from a cherishing of individualist values, but since it would in such an event have to qualify its imperative claims for freedom from legislative interference by a recognition of the individualist values which are injured by such freedom, its relations are likely to be solely empirical. The change from the individualism at the basis of the previous period of judicial toleration to the *laissez-faire* of the new restrictive period measured the difference between the two intellectual climates. There was of course a new alignment in the Court; the old minority had become a majority. But it was a new Court in a new society. It was not a sport, but an organic part of a period which has come down in the history of American life as thin in its cultural fiber and crass in its political morality. One may hazard that much of the responsibility is to be laid to the disillusioning effect of the competitive breakdown under the pressure of new and unscrupulous business *mores.*

The period of judicial toleration had, we have noted, been a crucial period, hesitant and divided when confronted by bewildering problems of a new industrialism. The period of judicial restriction was, when confronted by a dangerous revolt against the incidence of the new forms of capitalist enterprise,[1] decisive

and militant. And it was in its own way remarkably creative. On every important front of public policy it transformed the existing doctrine with considerable ingenuity[2]— in the field of railroad regulation . . . , business control . . . , federal taxation . . . , regulation of hours . . . , social legislation . . . , and anti-trust cases. . . . It was in this period that the powerful conceptions of contemporary constitutional law — due process, police powers, liberty of contract, and the rule of reasonableness — received their real impetus and elaboration.

In the past quarter-century the trend of judicial decision has again become vacillating for lack of some decisive movement within capitalist enterprise itself to give it firmness and direction. The second decade of the century is generally considered to have been "liberal," and *Muller v. Oregon* was hailed as a significant turning-point; the third decade is regarded as a "reactionary" return to normalcy; during the past several years liberals with their ears to the ground

[1] Not least among the causes for the militancy of the possessing classes, reflected in the militancy of the Court, was the influx of immigration and the growth of a labor movement which, while in the main a "business unionism" variety, was often engaged in violent clashes with employers. The fear of the immigrant worker, and the contempt for him have been influential in American history not only in heightening the clash between capitalists and laborers, but in putting behind the former a united body of opinion representing middle-class respectability. The Court in its decisions in this period reflected the prevalent Catonian attitude toward the labor movement, which called for its extirpation. I Commons, *op. cit. supra,* note 29, at 9, points out, however, that the courts by blocking labor's way toward reform

probably made the trade-union movement even more aggressive.

[2] The sequence of steps by which the Fourteenth Amendment was pressed into use for the protection of business interests against legislative regulation seems to have been somewhat as follows: (1) The decision that corporations are "persons" within the meaning of the amendment; (2) the decision that equal protection of the laws applies to foreign corporations as well as to individuals from outside states; (3) the decision that the due process clause applies to legislative and administrative attempts to regulate rates and other matters connected with the conduct of business enterprise; (4) the decision that liberty of contract is a right of liberty (or of property) within the meaning of the amendment; (5) the decision that the police power and the public interest doctrine must be narrowly and urgently construed in determining exemption from the due process clause; (6) the decision that the reasonableness of state legislation is not a matter of presumption by the fact that the legislation passed the gantlet of the legislative process, but is open to examination by the Court.

have again detected pulsations of hope. A closer analysis, however, of these three phases of the period fails to reveal any striking contrasts. Nor do they show a unified line of growth. At the bottom of their failure to achieve direction lies the character of the finance-capitalist society in which they have been working. Its pace of change in the field of both corporate and human relations has been too rapid to leave the earlier legal rules untouched, but too insecure to furnish a means of transforming them. It has ceased to be merely a monopoly capitalism, but it has not yet articulated a technique to control its new creatures, the giant corporation and the expanding credit structure. It has outgrown its complete imperviousness to the plight of the underlying classes, but has not yet found a way of meeting either their demands or their requirements. The old individualistic controls are clearly a thing of the past; to cling to them would involve drastic results for the entire economic structure. But pending discovery of controls that will replace them the Court has waited for a crystallization of capitalist attitudes. The tentativeness of this period has of course furnished the able and decisive minority group with a golden opportunity to influence the trend of decision. But a minority can work only interstitially, within the limits set by the dominant institutions, and never against the grain of current economic development. Whether capitalist enterprise can crystallize its new purposes and perfect its techniques sufficiently to give the Court again a clear faith and an articulated ideology remains to be seen.

The nexus between the course of Supreme Court decision and the realities of American capitalism poses some crucial problems as to the nature of the judicial process. It is upon this broader question that all our current theoretical interests in American constitutional law converge, for it is here that one approaches the dynamics of growth in the law. Contemporary American thought on this question is in the transitional stage attendant upon having shattered the old absolutes without having yet arrived at new formulations. It has rejected the rhetoric and the traditional mumbo-jumboism with which the reverent generations had invested the fundamental law. It finds it no longer possible to regard the judicial utterances as Delphic, and takes an almost irreverent delight in uncovering the bonds that link Supreme Court justices to other human beings. The myths have fallen away. But the absence of myths does not constitute theory; it is at best merely preparation for it.

It will be well to distinguish two aspects of contemporary thought on the Supreme Court and its economic relations. One has to do with the function that the Court decisions perform, the other with the forces determining them. The prevailing view of the function of the Court is thoroughly realistic. It sees the Court as a definite participant in the formation of public policy, often on matters of far-reaching economic and social importance. Viewed thus, the Court through its power to veto legislation has also the power to channel economic activity. In that sense it has been often called a super-legislature, exercising powers tantamount to the legislative power, but more dangerously, since it is not subject to the same popular control. The main contention here is sound, although the particular formulation it is given is often overstressed. Whether we shall call the Court a super-legislature or a super-judiciary has in reality only a propagandist relevance. Except from the viewpoint of a separation-of-powers ideal or a shattering of intellectual myths it is of little import. But what is of great import is the fact that the Court has become, through its exercise of the judicial power in the intricate context of contemporary capitalist society, a crucial agency of social control. As such it is part of our fabric of statesmanship and should be judged in terms of its effect upon American life.

The second aspect of the problem relates to an adequate theory of judicial decision. The contemporary trend is to regard each judge as acting upon his own economic beliefs and his own preferences as to social policy, and as rationalizing or deliberately manipulating his legal views into conformity with his social views. This represents of course an extreme revulsion against the traditional view of the judge as objectively expounding a body of law that has some superior truth-sanction. It looks toward a complete and perhaps unfruitful atomism: *tel juge, tel jugement*. It would hold that the course of judicial decision is the sum of the personal choices of the judges, and that the policy of the Court is determined at any time by the chance concatenation of nine arbitrary wills. Side by side with this there is another trend toward a sort of environmentalism or economic determinism. While holding to the atomistic view of the judicial process, it emphasizes in each judge not the volitional and whimsical elements but the non-volitional and determined. It examines his early life, education, economic affiliations, and property interests, and by a selective process with which every biographer is acquainted it shows the inevitable flow of what he is from what he has been. Both these approaches stress the compelling reality of the judge's views of social policy as over against his adherence to legal rules in

determining his decision; in this respect they mark a change from the tendency a decade or more ago to make the antithesis one between logic and experience, between a mechanical adherence to *stare decisis* and a realistic awareness of the changing needs of the day.

Such a theory of the judicial process obviously contains much that is sound and fruitful along with elements that tend to be merely impressionistic. Its atomism derives probably from influences similar to those which led Justice Cardozo to focus his analysis of the nature of the judicial process on the individual judge and the individual decision. Cardozo's discussion of the various intellectual procedures open to the judge comes dangerously close to a new Benthamism by which the isolated judge balances the compulsions of logic against the claims of philosophy and both against the persuasions of sociology. By a similar Benthamism in the current atomistic view the judge is made a lightning calculator not of competing intellectual methods but of his own desires and devices. Both views are helpful through their insistence that whatever influences the judicial decision must pass through the mind of the judge. But they do not take sufficient account of the fact that his mind is itself largely a social product, and that he is a judge within an economic system and an ideological milieu. Their influence is operative even when he is not applying the "method of sociology," or using law consciously as an instrument for social ends.

For the problem of the relation of capitalism to the Supreme Court the construction of a theory of judicial decision is of crucial importance. If the historical analysis presented in the last two sections is valid, much in the development of American constitutional law is explainable in terms of a developing capitalism. Such an influence, to be effective, would have had to be operative somehow on the minds of the judges, through whom alone constitutional law grows. But how? In what form and through what agencies have the effects of economic development been transmitted to the minds of the judges? The easiest answer of course would lie in a theory of pressures. But while this might be valid for some of the lower reaches of the American judiciary, it has no meaning at all for these men, who are placed by their exalted and permanent positions beyond the reach of corruption, as they are placed also beyond that of democratic control. A theory of interests is likely to be more valid. The judge is a member of an economic class, of a social grouping, of a geographical section. He shares their interests and will, even if unconsciously, direct his policy-forming function to their advantage. But unless this theory is broadened to include general ideological influences as well as direct interests, it will suffer from the over-simplified and mechanical interpretation that has been applied to the framing of the Constitution.

An adequate theory of the judicial process in the Supreme Court would have to take account of a number of factors. (1) The Court works first of all with a set of traditional and technical legal elements. It must stay within the framework of a Constitution, confine itself to the facts and issues of actual cases brought before it, observe and create for itself a body of procedure. It must maintain so much continuity with its own past decisions as to achieve the necessary minimum of legal certainty, and so much consistency with its own past reasonings as to make the body of constitutional law a somewhat orderly intellectual system.

In the process it creates concepts and develops doctrines, such as due process, liberty of contract, and police power, giving them thereby a directive force over its future decisions. There has been a tendency in recent thought to treat all these legal factors in the judicial process less as rules than as techniques — fairly flexible and accordingly subservient to the more deeply rooted purposes of the judges. (2) The Court works within a cultural and institutional framework which the justices share with their fellow-citizens. They live in and are sworn to preserve a society which is the end-product of a historical growth but is also changing under their very fingers. This society is dominated by its capitalist system of economic organization and is therefore best viewed as a capitalist society. Its institutions and modes of thought are partly incorporated in the Constitution, partly in the body of constitutional law, but are mainly resident in the life of the society itself. (3) The Court works in a world of ideas which the justices share with their fellow-men. These ideological elements — conceptions of human nature, human motive, social possibility, and ethical values — may be "preconceptions" and therefore submerged in consciousness, or they may be avowedly held and deliberately applied. Many of them, such as the competitive ideal and the right of property, proceed from the economic world; those that do not, such as human nature, individualism, and natural law, have nevertheless a definite bearing on economic problems; all of them are social products and are affected by changes in the social and economic structure. (4) There are personal and intellectual differences between the judges — differences of background, philosophy, social convictions, and sympathies.

Of these factors the second and third groups — the world of social fact and the world of social idea — include and are conditioned by the nature of our economic life. The selection that any particular judge makes of them will constitute what Thomas Reed Powell has called the "logic" of his decision; the selection that he makes of the first group of factors — the legal tradition and technology — will constitute the "rhetoric" by which he supports and rationalizes his decision. For an explanation of the main trend of constitutional decision we may therefore look to the institutional and ideological elements that exercise their compulsive force on the minds of the judges, and to the changes wrought in these elements principally by economic development. For an explanation of the groupings within the Court, we may look to the variations in outlook and belief as between the individual members.

This raises a question about the Court which is as important for social action as for juristic theory. What technique can be employed for shifting and controlling the trend of the Court's decisions? What are the chances, for example, that the Court will reverse the secular trend of its decisions during the past half-century and adopt an attitude toward private property that will tolerate experiments in the direction of a controlled and articulated economy? The contemporary emphasis on the judge's capacity to make his rhetoric march to the tune of his social beliefs has as corollary the view that the crucial concern, whether of liberals or conservatives, should be the selection of the right judges — a sort of eugenics program for the judicial process. It seems clear, however, that such a view is overoptimistic. It stops at the judge and does not push its analysis to

what it is that determines his view of life. The judge's convictions and social preferences run in terms of the current ideologies of his day; through those ideologies the operative economic forces and master trends of the period find their way into the Court's decisions. In such a sense it has been said that a period deserves whatever Supreme Court it gets — because it has created the judges in its own ideological image. A period in which capitalist enterprise is on the aggressive and the individualistic ideal sweeps everything before it is not likely to read anything but an individualistic philosophy into its constitutional law. A period such as the present, in which the individualistic ideal has been undermined by worldwide economic collapse, is likely to be increasingly tolerant of departures from an absolute conception of liberty or property.

This does not involve, however, a rigorous determinism, either economic or ideological. The judicial process is not, as a too mechanical view might hold, powerless in the clutch of capitalist circumstance. The current institutions and ways of thought of a period determine only the larger outlines which the constitutional law of the period is likely to take. Within that framework there is room for a fairly wide selection and variation of emphasis. The Supreme Court effects a nexus between our fundamental law and our fundamental economic institutions. But by its very position as an agency of control it is powerful to change the contours of those institutions. The same constitutional fabric that contains the absolute individualism of Justice Sutherland gives scope also to the humanistic individualism of Justice Holmes and the social constructivism of Justice Brandeis. The judicial process in the Supreme Court is no exception to the order of things everywhere. Within the limits set by its nature and function it can be carried on with creativeness and purpose or it can become merely a form of submission to the current drift. . . .

The Court's own *apologia* for its power — what may be called the "official" theory of the judicial function — is well known, but I shall take the liberty of recapitulating it. It runs somewhat as follows. We have a fundamental law, in the form of a written Constitution, overriding legislative enactments that are not in harmony with it. We have a federal system, in which powers must be divided between the states and the central government; and a system of separated powers, in which the lines must be drawn between the departments of the government, and the encroachments of one upon the others avoided. We have thus in two respects a system that would result in chaos or tyrannny unless there were a final arbiter. We have, moreover, the danger that men in power will aggrandize their power at the expense of other men, and invade their rights; we have a people safe from such invasion only under the protection of the Constitution. We have finally a judicial body, deliberately placed above politics and beyond partisan control, and empowered to assure for us a government of laws and not of men. The fund of knowledge and principles to which this body appeals is to be found in the Anglo-American common law, the precedents of constitutional law, and a "higher law" resident in the "genius of republican institutions."

In its way this official theory is something of a masterpiece. It is, to be sure, a mosaic pieced together from diverse materials: the *Federalist Papers,* Court decisions and dicta, commentaries by scholars such as Kent and Cooley, classic speeches such as those of Webster; but, while it is a mosaic, it is a thing of beauty nevertheless, neat, logical, close-fitting, comprehensive — so long as you grant its premises.

Let me set out some of those premises, generally unexpressed. The official theory assumes that a fundamental law must be superior to all legislative enactments, despite the example of the English system, where the line of constitutional growth lies in parliamentary enactment rather than judicial construction. It assumes that other departments of the government may not be as capable as the judiciary of the task of constitutional construction — assumes, that is, a fund of exclusive and inspired knowledge of the law on the part of the judges. It assumes that the binding obligation of a litigant at law to accept the Court's construction of a statute is binding as well upon Congress. It assumes on the part of the executive and the legislature an imperialistic thirst for power and expansion, and despite Justice Stone's agonizing cry *de profundis* in the Butler case ("the only check upon our own exercise of power is our own sense of self-restraint"), despite this cry, the official theory makes no similar assumption about the stake the judges have in their own power. It assumes that all government is dangerous, and thus adopts a negativist attitude toward governmental powers. It assumes that the legal aspects of a governmental problem can be separated and abstracted from its real aspects. It assumes, in short, a closed Constitution in a malignant universe, instead of an open instrument of government in a changing and challenging world.

I have spoken thus far of the formal ideology of the judicial power. But an ideology is not merely a series of linked propositions drawn from related premises. It sometimes draws its greatest strength from allies — ideas in this case not directly within the official *apologia* of the Court's power, but embedded in the popular mind and strengthening the acceptance of that power. I want to pick four of them for brief discussion — the doctrine of limited governmental powers, the doctrine of the sanctity of property, the doctrine of federalism, and the doctrine of minority rights.

The Constitution was born in a century obsessed with the notion of limited powers, a century overhung by the shadows of Locke and Rousseau. Conservative thought clung to the rights of minorities against the tyranny of the majority; and radical theory, such as that of Jefferson and the great European rationalists, took the form of belief in the perfectibility of man and the malignancy of government. But the pattern of the century contained a curious inner contradiction in its thought. Its prevailing economic policy was mercantilistic, with all the close and comprehensive controls that the mercantilist state exercised over economic life, and with all its resulting concentration of authority. Its prevailing political thought, however, was atomistic, with its emphasis on individual liberties and governmental dangers. The men who framed the Constitution and ran the government that it created were caught in this contradiction. Their conservative economic interests dictated a strong central mercantilist government; the prevailing political ideas of the time, fortifying their fear of democracy, made them place that government of expanded powers in an intellectual framework of limited powers. Hence, to a large extent, the confusion of the Constitutional debates. The interesting fact is that judicial ideology still clings to this doctrine even in a world where to act on it would be grotesquely tragic, and where the popular impulse is to abandon it.

When we pass to the doctrine of the sanctity of property, we find that the sense of property has assumed a variety of forms in our history, but always the protection and support it has accorded to the judicial power has been a continuing factor in the Court's life. American life has pushed forward along a variety of trails — farm, frontier, and factory; plantation and city; trade route, logging-camp, mining-town, and real-estate boom; corporation and co-operative. But through all these the common base-line has been a persistent and pervasive sense of property. It first took the form of the land-mysticism and land-hunger of Physiocratic thought, deeply resident in the whole movement of colonial land-settlement, and from which Jefferson eventually drew much of his support; then the sense of vested rights and the deep sense of contractual obligation, to which Marshall gave doctrinal expression in his "contract decisions," and which, using and twisting somewhat Sir Henry Sumner Maine's terminology, provided a new sort of status for an age of capitalism; then the sense of property individualism, born of the movements for European liberation, blessed with the approval of Protestant capitalism, flourishing in the wilderness of the American frontier, turned into *laissez-faire* by the conditions of a reckless and exploitative capitalism; and finally, when individualism could no longer thrive as an idea because it had been extinguished as a fact in economic life, the clinging to the profit system and the cash-nexus as bulwarks against social anarchy and the destruction of the social fabric. This sense of property, even when its widespread social base has been so largely destroyed in the age of absentee ownership, is still a powerful ally for the judicial power.

When we turn to the theory of federalism and states' rights, we are dealing with a powerful intellectual and sentimental force that the Supreme Court has at times had to fight and more latterly has been calling to its aid. We are all acquainted with the kinds of arguments which, like ghosts, are continually looming up in the world of ideas, which rule us from the past by their wraith-like being, although we are aware that they no longer represent actualities. The idea of free opportunity under capitalism is one, and it lingers on even in a world dominated by monopoly. In the political realm the most potent and assertive American ghost is still federalism. Most of its former functions have been stripped from it; it haunts a nation in which every force drives toward centralization, both economic and political. But when I call it a ghost, I do not mean it is no longer a fact to be reckoned with. The strength of a ghost, it must be remembered, rests in its capacity to get itself believed; and that, in turn, depends more than anything on our own needs and fears. And the fear of overcentralization, of the wiping out of the traditional political and cultural landmarks of the states, is a very real fear, especially in the light of what the fascist dictatorships have done to federalism. And it is a fear which the Supreme Court, as witness the AAA case, has not been averse to exploring and exploiting.

It may be said of the doctrine of minority rights and individual liberties that recent events have given them or seem to have given them even greater meaning than they once possessed. This tradition of minority rights has always been an important source of strength for judicial supremacy. The doctrine of vested rights, the sanctity of contract and liberty of contract, the doctrine of due process of law — all have drawn upon this tradition. In fact, most of the Court's decisions invalidating legislation hostile to property might be interpreted as proceeding from its zeal for minority rights, rather than from any untoward zeal for business interests. Nevertheless, as long as a strong rationalization for capitalist power existed in economic thought and opinion, the civil-liberties and minority-rights argument was secondary. Now, however, two things are happening to push it to the fore. One is the decline of *laissez-faire*, both in practice and in thought. The second is the spread of fascism in Europe and the fear of it in America. The first has made the businessmen and the judges turn increasingly to the rhetoric of civil liberties; the second has made the liberals and the middle classes more ready to accept the Court's guardianship of civil liberties, even if it means a measure of judicial control over economic policy.

About civil liberties and minority rights and the liberals I shall have more to say later. But I want to pause here for a moment to survey the meaning of these four ideological allies of the judicial power. All four, viewed historically, have their roots in majority movements, and have played a great and even revolutionary role in the history of the Western World. And all four have been turned to the uses of minority rule as parts of the constitutional tradition. Take, first, the idea of a government of limited powers. The notion of a higher law; the idea of natural rights of individuals, which adhere to them independently of government and even in despite of government.

and which must be protected against government; the necessity of disobedience to a government that violated these rights — these had once been living parts of a revolutionary movement that swept Western Europe from the parliamentary champions of the struggle against the Tudors and Stuarts to the philosophers of the French Revolution. They were majority movements, aimed at limiting the powers of minority governments of the dying classes. They rationalized the actual movement toward parliamentarism in England and toward middle-class democracy in France. But in taking them over, judicial review turned them to quite different uses — to defeat parliamentary supremacy and hedge democracy around with severe limitations — in short, to the uses of minority rule. And the same may be said of that property sense which has been part of the American democratic experience, of the democratic localism that underlies federalism and states' rights, and of the democratic movements that generated the doctrines of civil liberties and minority rights. All have been twisted out of their original context, and turned to the uses of minority rule.

I want now to examine more closely what I mean by three concepts I have been using — democracy (or majority will), minority rule, and minority rights. The relation between these three is central to an understanding of the ideology of the judicial power.

Scratch a fervent believer in judicial supremacy, and like as not you will find someone with a bitterness about democracy. The two are as close as skin and skeleton. When I speak of *democracy* here, I want to distinguish it sharply from *liberalism*. There is no greater confusion in the layman's mind today than the tendency to identify the two. American history has been the scene of a protracted struggle between democratic and anti-democratic forces. Anti-democracy began as aristocratic thought, with emphasis on a neo-Greek élite. Alexander Hamilton, heart-broken because the new American state could not be a monarchy with George Washington as king and himself as king-maker, sublimated his monarchical passion in a dream of America as an aristocracy of property. And a whole school followed him. But it soon became clear that in a country where a revolutionary war had been fought to achieve democracy, an aristocratic body of thought could not form the base of any party successful at the polls. The collapse of the Federalist Party proved it.

A shift was made, therefore, to liberalism; and so powerful an aid did liberalism become to the anti-democratic forces that even conservatism grew shamefaced, and, in order to survive, had to don the garments of liberalism. In the South alone, in the period of tension preceding the Civil War, slavery as an economic base caused aristocratic theory to linger on, and the spokesmen for the slavocracy defended it as an élite that had re-established a Greek republic among the roses and cotton bolls below the Mason-Dixon line. But the Civil War proved by blood and iron that aristocratic theory was, like slavery, an unnecessary survival from archaic times. The northern financial oligarchy that rose to unchallenged political power out of the Civil War spoke thereafter in the name of an orthodox, if slightly cynical, liberalism. And it has continued to do so.

Let us be clear about it; minority-rights liberalism (which becomes in practice minority-rule liberalism) furnishes the only reasoned defense of the capitalist power that we have in America. This liberalism has three facets: a defense of individual civil liberties against society, a defense of minority rights (including both human and property rights) against the possible tyranny of the government, and a belief in rationalism and in the final triumph of the idea. In the course of the liberal revolutions in Europe, democratic forces were unleashed which sought to carry the implications of the libertarian movements to their logical conclusion not only for the middle class but for the underlying population as well, not only for political but for economic freedom and equality. These forces are what I shall call the "democratic impetus" or the "democratic thrust." They began to loom as the great threat to the privileged position of the middle classes. Fortunately for those classes, they could find in the armory of liberalism the intellectual weapons they needed for fighting the democratic threat. The basis of democracy is that the majority will shall prevail; its premise is that the common man can fashion his own political destiny, and that government must consist of representative institutions to carry the majority will into execution. To this, liberalism has opposed the proposition that the freedom and rights of the individual and the minority were more sacred than the will of the majority. In that lies the essential distinction between liberalism and democracy.

In their fear of majority will the propertied groups have depicted the democratic mass movements in the darkest colors of extremism. They have called the Jeffersonians "Jacobins," the Jacksonians "Locofocs," the Abolitionists "Niggerlovers," the agrarian radicals "Populists," the trade unionists "Reds" and "Bolsheviks." The democratic forces in turn have responded by calling the propertied groups "Monarchists," "plutocrats," "economic royalists." The two barrages of epithets have enlivened American poli-

tics, but failed to illuminate it. But behind the battle of the epithets there has been a very real struggle between the thrust of majority will, ever present in a nation whose collective life has been based on democratic premises, and the counter-thrust of minority rule.

This has been the basic paradox of American life — the necessity we have been under of squaring majority will with minority rule — that is, democratic forms with capitalist power. It has made us, in one sense, politically speaking, a nation of hypocrites. But it has also spurred our wits and sharpened the edge of our political inventiveness. Out of it have emerged our peculiar institution of judicial supremacy and that whole idea structure of the defense of judicial supremacy which I have outlined.

The mistake we are all too ready to make is to pose an antithesis between the Constitution as such and the democratic impulse, an antithesis that does not exist. We have been led into this error partly by the excellent work of Charles Beard and his school in proving that the Constitution represented the property interests of the minority. That is true enough. But we must also remember that the Constitution, without the accretion of judicial review, could (whatever its origins) have become an instrument of the majority will. The whole animus behind it, despite the system of checks and balances was a flexible one. It was meant, as has recently been pointed out with great effectiveness by Professor Hamilton and Professor Corwin, to adapt itself to the changes and chances of national life. It is significant that the majority groups, who were first rather sullen about it, and then accepted it after affixing to it a bill of rights guaranteeing individual liberties, finally became enthusiastic about it. It is well known that

Jeffersonians as well as Hamiltonians and Marshallians vied in their praise of the Constitution. What they differed about was the judicial power. The real antithesis is between the democratic impulse and the judicial power. And with Jefferson and the so-called Revolution of 1800, which saw the triumph of Jeffersonianism, began that series of democratic thrusts, upsurges of the majority will, that has enlivened and vitalized American history. In Jefferson and Jackson, notably in the Bank War and the Dorr Rebellion, in Lincoln, to an extent in Cleveland, in the Populist movement and Bryan, in Theodore Roosevelt and Woodrow Wilson, in Eugene Debs, in Franklin Roosevelt and the New Deal, and in John L. Lewis and the CIO, we have had repetitions of that democratic thrust at the seats of minority power. It became the task of the propertied minority to ward off those thrusts. And they have been thus far enabled to do it through the instrument of judicial supremacy, the ideology that surrounds and defends it, and especially the ideology of liberalism.

In two senses judicial supremacy has smoothed the way for minority rule. In one specific instance after another, measures of policy which the majority has desired have been invalidated by the courts. If the people of Georgia wanted to undo a corrupt grant of land, or the people of New York wanted an eight-hour working day in bakery shops, or the people of Oklahoma wanted to restrict the number of ice-plants, their wishes were so much dry stubble to be trod under foot by the minority will of the Court.

But there is an even deeper sense in which the Supreme Court has acted as the final barricade against the assaults of democratic majorities. We must remember that the process of the triumph of the democratic majority is a long and tedious process, as majority leaders from Jefferson to Franklin Roosevelt have discovered. It is a process of seeking to displace the enemy from one position after another. There is the vast inertia of the party system, with an autonomous force of its own even after popular sentiment has changed; there is the political apathy of the masses, the tendency they have of forgetting to remember. There is the pressure of special interests, blocking up committees, arranging filibusters. There is the control that the vested interests exercise over our newspapers and our very patterns of thinking. And there is, finally, the effective weapon the propertied minority has in withdrawing capital from investment and thus paralyzing the economic process. And after all these positions have been captured, the anti-democratic forces retreat to their last barricade — judicial review. There, behind the safe earthworks of natural law, due process, minority rights, the judges can in the plenitude of their virtue and sincerity veto and outlaw the basic social program of the majority.

The democratic forces of the country have known, in intervals of lucidity, what they were up against and what they were fighting. But in addition to all the difficulties of mustering the necessary big electoral battalions, they have become increasingly confused recently. And their confusion has arisen from the fact that the rationalizations that are used to explain and defend the Supreme Court power are the rationalizations that flow from the premises of liberalism — that minority rule uses the theory of minority rights, and manages somehow to equate the two.

Minority rule has recently had to work very subtly to defeat majority will. There was a time, in Alexander Hamilton's day, when the anti-democratic theorists could say frankly, when confronted with the accusation that they had defeated the people's will: "Your people, Sir, is a great beast." Or they could speak more gravely, as did Fisher Ames, of "a government of the wise, the rich, and the good," as if all three were coterminous. Later they had to convert the Bill of Rights and the Fourteenth Amendment, the heart of the protection of minority rights, from a charter of liberties to a charter of property protection. The task, as is well known, was a difficult one, and involved two major intellectual somersaults — twisting due process of law from a procedural meaning to a substantive meaning, and endowing the corporation with all the attributes of human personality. But, while the task was well done, it was done with a certain cynicism that is particularly apparent in the political commentaries between the Civil War and the World War, as well as in the Court decisions of that period. Now, however, in the midst of world tensions in which democracy has taken on a new meaning and a new prestige for us, it is necessary to be more subtle in defense of minority rule. The new defense is, therefore, not only a plea of minority rights, powerfully evocative in itself in these days, but a new interpretation of majority will as well.

That interpretation is to be found in its most finished form not in the Supreme Court decisions, in all of which it is implicit, nor even in scholarly commentary, but in two popular commentators, Mr. Walter Lippmann and Miss Dorothy Thompson. It is significant that Mr. Lippmann embodies it in his book *The Good Society*, which is an attack on economic planning, the most dangerous threat to the economic power of the minority. It is even more significant that Miss Thompson's theory, which is the more sharply delineated, is to be found

best in a series of three articles which form a critique of Mr. Roosevelt's Roanoke Island speech.

The new theory (I use Miss Thompson's articles as a model) reinterprets the democratic principle so that it becomes something quite different from the naked principle of majority will. First, not only must minorities be protected from majorities, but majorities must even be protected from themselves. Second, if true democracy does operate in terms of majority will, it is not the will of a numerical majority, but a very different conception. Third, the notion of numerical majorities really smells of fascism. And having arrived at that position, one falls back in fright on minority rights, even if it involves scrapping the TVA, the Wagner Act, the Securities and Exchange Commission, and the Labor Relations Board.

When we say that majorities must be protected from themselves, the premise is the anti-democratic one — that the common man may be good material for being ruled but that he has no capacity for governing. When we go on to talk of "true" democracy, as distinguished from majority will, what are we saying? We are saying that democracy is nothing so vulgar and demagogic as a counting of heads, but that there is a "real" national will, as distinguished from the one that expresses itself at the polls. That real national will is somehow a trusteeship of the minority. For the few know what is to the interest of the many better than the many know themselves. This whole conception of the national will as something transcending numbers and having no traffic with the felt desires of the day is an essentially mystical conception.

It has always been the role of reactionary thought to retreat to a mystical conception of the body politic, as witness Burke, de Maistre, Adam Müller, and the

French Catholic school. For mystical notions enable you to escape from the fact of the naked majority will. And conservative minority groups have always regarded the majority as unsavory, as meaningless by the very fact of numbers, strident and mechanical like the clashing of weapons through which the primitive Germanic tribes indicated their assent by the greatest noise. What is novel is the fact that all this is now said — and believed — in the name of liberalism. And yet not so novel if we consider the extent to which the ingredients of liberal thinking — that is, minority-rule thinking — have entered into the traditional defense of the judicial power under the Constitution.

What has happened, of course, cannot be blamed on the Constitution. What has happened is that there has been built in America an extra-democratic structure of economic reality which dare not operate through the democratic machinery; for the democratic machinery is too easily turned into an instrument for leveling economic privilege. When this extra-democratic structure of economic reality (I use it as an academic phrase for the structure of corporate power) is challenged, and a successful attempt is made to take our democratic theory literally and nakedly, how far will the corporate groups allow this attempt to go? To my mind, this is the most important question that the Constitution faces in the calculable future, and it faces it more dangerously than it has confronted any problem since the Civil War. Does the economic interest of the corporate groups so far outweigh their sense of commonwealth as to make them ready either to keep their minority rule or scrap the whole democratic framework? My own conviction is that this is their attitude, and that they will insist on one or the other of these alternatives. When the corporation cannot win its fight against democracy by economic means, it may call in military and political means and become (if I may give the term a twist) the corporative state.

If this is so, the new attack on the majority principle, represented by Miss Thompson and Mr. Lippmann, takes on a disquieting importance. A counterthrust against a successful labor government, for example, will look for a theory to attach itself to. Here is a theory readymade. The naked majority principle, Miss Thompson tells us, is really fascist; it is part of a totalitarian state. I find a readiness in surprisingly intelligent quarters to accept this paradox. If that readiness spreads, corporate power will not lack those intellectual garments which it needs to stave off a socialized democracy — intellectual garments which the liberals are now spinning just as assiduously as the Parcae once spun other fateful garments.

1938

Robert E. Cushman:

THE SUPREME COURT
AND THE CONSTITUTION

THE average citizen has a very whole-some respect for the Constitution of the United States. His respect does not usually come from any clear or accurate knowledge of the document itself, but grows out of the belief that the Constitution sanctions those policies which he approves and forbids those which seem to him dangerous or oppressive. His reaction to the Supreme Court is similarly direct and forthright; its decisions are sound if he likes them and unsound if he does not. While this solution of our constitutional problems by the "hunch" method has the advantage of simplicity, it is rather too simple to be helpful in answering two very vital questions now before the country: (1) Is our Constitution adequate to the demands of our present day national life? (2) Is the Supreme Court preserving our Constitution or obstructing its normal and healthy expansion?

It is well to remember that the "fathers" who framed the Constitution were no more competent to manage their affairs than we are to manage ours. They relied upon what political experience they had, but much of their work was frankly experimental. Some parts of the Constitution in which they took the greatest pride, such as the intricate method of electing the President, failed completely to work as they intended.

Certain inadequacies in the original document, as interpreted by the Supreme Court, had to be met by constitutional amendments. But the basic features of the Constitution of 1936 are those of the Constitution of 1787. For purposes of the present discussion those basic features may be summed up as follows:

1. The Constitution set up the outlines of a structure of national government, while at the same time it left intact the state governments.

2. The Constitution worked out a division of powers between the new national government and the states. It did this by delegating to the new national government the powers deemed necessary for national purposes, and by declaring that the powers not thus given to the new nation were left to the states unless specifically forbidden to them. The national government had only the powers positively given to it; the states kept all the powers not taken away from them.

3. The Constitution, with its added amendments, carefully listed certain vital civil liberties which the new federal government might not invade. Most of these were set out in the Bill of Rights added in 1790. Other guarantees of civil liberty were set up as limitations upon the states. Here we find prohibition against impairment of the obligation of contracts and later the all-important due process and

Robert E. Cushman, *The Supreme Court and the Constitution* (Public Affairs Pamphlet, No. 7, 1936), pp. 1–36. Used by permission.

equal protection clauses of the Four-teenth Amendment.

4. The new Constitution declared it-self to be the "supreme law of the land," a fundamental law binding upon state and federal officers alike. To make effec-tive this concept of the Constitution, the Supreme Court, after putting out one or two hesitant feelers, boldly announced in 1803 in the case of Marbury *v.* Madison[1] that it was the organ of government to maintain the supremacy of the Constitu-tion and that in the exercise of its judicial work of applying the law in cases brought before it, it would invalidate acts of Con-gress which were in conflict with the Constitution. Since the Constitution it-self declared its supremacy over conflict-ing state legislation, the power of the Supreme Court to invalidate state laws deemed to violate that Constitution was even easier to defend. Whether the fram-ers of the Constitution intended the Su-preme Court to exercise this power of "judicial review" in enforcing the su-premacy of the Constitution, or whether the Court "usurped" it, has evoked bitter argument which we need not enter into here. Whether "usurped" or not, and the weight of historical argument is against the charge of "usurpation," the Supreme Court has exercised this important power of declaring statutes unconstitutional ever since Marshall established the precedent in 1803, and it is now as much a part of the working American Constitution as the provision that Senators shall be chosen for six years or that the President may veto bills sent to him by Congress.

Nation Changed since 1789

Thus the basic nature of our constitu-tional system has not changed since 1789.

[1] 1 Cranch 137.

But the nation which it governs has vastly changed. From a fringe of jealous and struggling colonies on the Atlantic seaboard it has become a great conti-nental empire, national in its thinking and its impulses, with an economic life pulsating through nationwide systems of markets, transportation, and communica-tions. Congress still has its delegated power to regulate commerce, and we are told that the power is unchanged; but what a difference between the commerce of 1787 and 1936! And so with the other delegated powers: they have not shrunk, they have not expanded, but they apply to concrete problems and situations be-yond the wildest imagination of the founding fathers.

This is also true of the guarantees of civil liberty found in the Constitution. No longer do they restrict the simple activities of an 18th century government, but they are used to measure the validity of the many complex rules and restric-tions which the modern nation and state impose upon the daily life of the citizen. What many thoughtful people have been asking is: How adequate is the old Con-stitution to the needs of a 20th century nation? Are the delegated powers broad enough to permit the federal government to deal with all truly national problems? Are the old limitations in behalf of civil liberty too strict or too loose? To what extent has the Supreme Court in constru-ing the Constitution been able to adapt its provisions to the demands of modern life? If the Constitution, as interpreted by the Court, prevents the proper solu-tion of our social and economic prob-lems, should we do something to the Constitution to meet the difficulty, or should we do something to the Supreme Court? . . .

PROPOSALS FOR CONSTITUTIONAL OR JUDICIAL REFORM

Whatever we may feel about the wisdom of the statutes involved it is a sobering thought that Congress cannot proceed with its program for agricultural rehabilitation because six of our nine Supreme Court justices so rule, and that neither the nation nor the states can protect women and children from starvation wages because five of the same nine justices find something in the words "due process of law" which prevents it. And this pushes to the front the question whether, viewing the whole situation, we think something ought to be done about it. And if we assume that something ought to be done, that raises a whole row of questions as to what can be done. Let us, then, examine the various positions which an intelligent citizen might take on this important question and see what ways are open to him to make his views effective.

1. In the first place there is the viewpoint that the Constitution is fully adequate to present day needs and that the Supreme Court is performing wisely and efficiently its difficult task of interpreting it. Those holding this opinion, and there are many, will naturally propose no changes in our constitutional or judicial system, but will, on the contrary, fight any changes that may be proposed.

2. In the second place there are those who view with concern the whole constitutional picture presented in the earlier pages but who feel that no change in the Constitution is needed and that any "tinkering" with the Supreme Court will be dangerous and unsatisfactory. These critics of the present system believe that the Constitution with its broad and generous clauses is sufficiently flexible to meet the changing demands of the modern nation. That flexibility must be rec-

ognized and accepted by the Supreme Court in the work of constitutional construction. And we must "educate" the Court through criticism, public discussion, and the various techniques of an informed public opinion to a more enlightened view of their task. A person thus minded is apt to quote Mr. Dooley's comment that the Supreme Court follows the election returns and, if more fully informed, alludes to the fact that the Supreme Court has actually reversed or drastically modified its decisions in about forty cases.[2] This shows that judicial opinions can be and sometimes are changed gradually and it is urged that such a process of evolution and adjustment is likely to be more satisfactory than any jerky and uncertain results attained by altering either the Constitution or the Court. In reply it is urged that few, if any reversals of the decisions of the Court have come about in answer to any immediately expressed public opinion, that the recent decisions indicate a trend toward judicial ruthlessness rather than judicial tolerance of legislative policies, and that such a program of judicial education is at best slow and uncertain. This, however, is no valid argument against employing the method as vigorously as possible in the hope of securing substantial results.

3. A third position is that the Constitution, properly interpreted, is fully adequate to our present day national needs, that the Supreme Court is at fault either in assuming the vast power it exercises, or in the way in which it uses it, and that we should, therefore, let the Constitution alone and reform the Court. Having

[2] These are listed in a footnote in a dissenting opinion by Mr. Justice Brandeis in Burner *v.* Coronado Oil and Gas Co. (1932), 285 U. S. 393.

agreed that something ought to be done to the Court, these reformers split up into at least five groups on the question of what to do.

"Packing" the Court

One thing that can be done to the Court is to "pack" it. By this is meant to increase the number of judges on the Court and fill the new places with men who have a more "liberal" point of view. For those who like speedy action this plan has the advantage of getting immediate results and of being a change which can be made by Congress without the aid of a constitutional amendment. The Constitution provides that there shall be a Supreme Court but leaves it to Congress to determine its size by statute. We started out with six justices, we have had as many as ten, and since 1869 we have had nine. There is no constitutional reason why we should not have fifteen or twenty-five. This scheme to "pack" the Court has a certain child-like simplicity. If we have judges whom we regard as bad, let us add to the Court enough good judges to outvote the bad ones and all will be well.

In 1870 the Supreme Court declared the Legal Tender Act invalid by a vote of four to three.[3] There were two vacancies on the Court at the time. President Grant filled these places with two men who promptly voted with the minority of three to reverse the decision by a vote of five to four.[4] Historians still argue as to whether Grant "packed" the Court, a question which we are not called upon to settle. It is more important to note that the incident cost the Court heavily in public confidence. Mr. Hughes calls the reversal under these circumstances "a self-inflicted wound." Those who urge that we "pack" the Supreme Court should bear in mind that packing may well be a two-edged sword. If we "pack" the Court with liberals there is nothing to prevent reprisal by the conservatives when they come into power, and the process may go on until all sound traditions of judicial independence are undermined. Furthermore, the packing of the Court with justices of a particular breed or color of view promises very uncertain results. If these men are really the kind whose judicial work will be directly governed by their political and economic affiliations, who will in short live up to the implied understanding which led to their appointment, they would appear to be unfit for judicial service. Nothing but calamity can be expected from a definitely biased Court. If, on the other hand, judicially-minded men are appointed in the expectation that their known predilections and hunches will color their work on the bench, it should be noted that experience does not bear this out sufficiently to make the method a very reliable instrument of specific reform. The history of the Supreme Court is full of cases in which Presidents appointed men to the bench in the hope that they would give effect to a certain point of view. Such efforts were almost always disappointing in their results. In virtually every case the justice so appointed failed to do his "duty" in this regard and settled down to be a judge and not a partisan.

But it is not necessary to swamp the Court in order to change its personnel. Five justices are now over seventy-four years of age and a sixth is over seventy.[5] The President elected in 1936 will hardly

---

[3] Hepburn *v.* Griswold (1870), 8 Wallace 603.

[4] Legal Tender Cases (1871), 12 Wallace 457.

[5] The ages of the justices are as follows: Hughes 74, Van Devanter 77, McReynolds 74, Brandeis 80, Sutherland 74, Butler 70, Stone 64, Roberts 61, Cardozo 66. The average age is 71.

escape the responsibility of appointing one or more justices. In doing so he will affect the trend of the Court's decisions for many years. If he appoints men with the broad judicial tolerance of a Brandeis, Stone, or Cardozo, the Constitution may prove flexible enough to meet the demands we are making on it. If he appoints hard-minded judicial dogmatists from the ultra-conservative school, we may find ourselves facing the issue of drastic constitutional revision. Those who believe the Constitution is adequate to our present needs, if flexibly construed, will do well to exert every ounce of influence toward the selection of justices who share their views, not on specific questions, but on the broad principles of liberal construction.

Limiting the Court's Jurisdiction

Another quick and easy method of dealing with the Supreme Court is to deprive it of its jurisdiction to decide cases in which constitutional questions are most likely to arise. This also may be done by act of Congress without amending the Constitution. Many who favor this plan are not wholly sure of their ground and are prone to lose track of certain basic facts. The Supreme Court has two kinds of jurisdiction, original and appellate. The original jurisdiction of the Supreme Court is fixed by the Constitution and cannot be increased or diminished by Congress. But that original jurisdiction does not figure in our present problem since it includes only cases affecting ambassadors, ministers and consuls, and cases between states of the union. The appellate jurisdiction of the Supreme Court, however, while it cannot be enlarged by Congress beyond the limits set forth in the Constitution, can be cut down or even abolished by statute.

The Constitution plainly states that such appellate jurisdiction shall be exercised subject to "such exceptions and under such regulations as the Congress shall make."

Congress has frequently changed this appellate jurisdiction, sometimes extending it and sometimes cutting it down. In one notable case Congress cut off the Court's appellate jurisdiction for the admitted purpose of preventing a decision on a constitutional question. This was the famous case of *ex parte* McCardle decided in 1869.[6] The case had already been argued in the Supreme Court on a question involving the constitutionality of the Reconstruction Act of 1867, an act which Congress had reason to suppose the Court might hold void. Before the Court could render a decision (although there is some evidence that the Court delayed to permit Congress to act) Congress repealed the statute giving the Court jurisdiction to hear the case on appeal. The Court decided that Congress had the power to do this and dismissed the case forthwith. Congress could constitutionally take from the Supreme Court all appellate jurisdiction, although this would leave a very peculiar judicial system. Or Congress could lop off the appellate jurisdiction of the Court in particular kinds of cases as it did when it made the jurisdiction of the Circuit Courts of Appeals final in all federal criminal cases not involving constitutional questions. But this vitally important fact must be kept in mind. As long as the Supreme Court is left with *any appellate jurisdiction whatever, Congress cannot constitutionally keep the Court from passing upon the validity of acts of Congress in any and all cases lying within that*

6 7 Wallace 506.

jurisdiction in which such constitutional questions can possibly arise.

Let us see why this is true. There is a difference between the jurisdiction of the Supreme Court and the judicial power exercised inside that jurisdiction. The actual substantive power which the United States Courts exercise is the "judicial power of the United States," and this they get from the Constitution, and not from Congress. The jurisdiction of the Courts, on the other hand, is the area of enclosure within which the judicial power is exercised. A federal judge put it very neatly when he said:[7]

We see that Congress . . . can as a potter shape the vessel of jurisdiction, that is, the capacity to receive, but having been made, the judicial power of the United States is poured into the vessel not by Congress but by the Constitution.

Congress, in other words, can determine whether the Supreme Court shall have any cases to decide on appeal, but if it allows it to decide any at all, it has nothing to say about the nature of the judicial power exercised in deciding them. Now the power of the Supreme Court of the United States to pass on the validity of laws (and the same is true of lower federal courts as well) *is an inherent element of the judicial power of the United States.* That is the orthodox theory of judicial review. That being true the power of judicial review cannot be impaired or taken away by Congress. Congress does not confer it and may not destroy it. That power, therefore, will still be exercised by the Supreme Court, and every other federal court, within the limits of any jurisdiction, however small, that Congress may permit these courts to exercise. Congress can prevent the Court

[7] Michaelson *v.* United States (1923), 291 Federal Reporter 940, 946.

from exercising judicial review of legislation only at the price of cutting off its power to exercise all judicial power. It follows that any legislative tampering with the appellate jurisdiction of the Supreme Court is a very left-handed and unsatisfactory method of dealing with the power which the courts exercise in construing the Constitution.

Preventing Five-to-Four Decisions

Still another proposal for "reforming" the Court is to provide that no act of Congress shall be invalidated by the Supreme Court unless seven of the nine justices agree. There is no sanctity about seven as the required majority, but that is the number most commonly proposed. Since this would be a change in the Court's exercise of its judicial power, rather than its jurisdiction, it would probably be necessary to amend the Constitution in order to bring it about, although there are able constitutional lawyers who believe that Congress could make this change by statute. This proposal is aimed at the evil of five-to-four decisions and has been strongly urged from time to time. Its underlying philosophy is simple and plausible. It is an accepted principle of constitutional construction that an act of Congress is presumed to be constitutional and should not be held void unless its invalidity is beyond all reasonable doubt. It is ridiculous, urge the advocates of this seven-to-two requirement, to say that a statute is void beyond reasonable doubt when four judges or even three believe it to be valid. If the constitutional issue is as close as that, the judgment of Congress should be upheld. Such a rule (the concurrence of seven judges) would have saved the A.A.A., the Guffey Act, the Railroad Retirement Act (on its broader merits), and the

Municipal Bankruptcy Act. It would not have saved the N.R.A. or the Frazier-Lemke Act.

Let us examine the plan more closely. Does not the "reasonable doubt" argument, in the form used, prove too much? All the courts have ever meant in saying that the unconstitutionality of a statute should be free from reasonable doubt before the act is held void, is that there should be no reasonable doubt in the minds of the judge or judges rendering the decision. Mr. Justice Roberts ought not to hold the A.A.A. void if he has doubts about its invalidity; but if he is not doubtful why should he vote to uphold it because Mr. Justice Stone has doubts, or believes it valid? There will always be some doubt somewhere or there would be no issue in the first place. This is the reason why a court which claims to be governed by the "reasonable doubt" test of validity continues to hand down five-to-four decisions. It does not, however, prove that we ought not to prevent such decisions. The seven-to-two rule might increase public confidence in the decisions of the Court and allay resentment. Exasperation at a decision one does not like is increased when it is a five-to-four decision. Then there is the other side of the picture which would appear when an act of Congress, attacked as invalid, is upheld and enforced when six members of the Court believe it to be unconstitutional. That would hardly produce widespread confidence in such a decision. It seems probable that more acts of Congress would be upheld than at present. Which ones they would be could not, of course, be foretold. The results of the rule would be neither very serious nor very helpful; but it is doubtful if they would be important enough to warrant passing a constitutional amendment.

Overriding the Court by Two-Thirds Vote of Congress

A much more drastic change in the power of the Supreme Court would be made by those who propose that decisions of the Supreme Court holding acts of Congress invalid could be overridden by a two-thirds vote of both houses of Congress. If this were done the act would be in effect in spite of the Court's decision. This is substantially the scheme advocated by the late Senator LaFollette in his campaign for the Presidency in 1924. This appears to be a sort of short-cut method of amending the Constitution on particular points brought up in particular cases. It reads into the Constitution the congressional construction embodied in the statute. It differs from the normal method of amending the Constitution in several ways. In the first place it permits amendment of the Constitution without ratification of the states. Take a concrete example. Congress passes a law making it a federal felony to participate in a lynching. This is the exercise of a power not delegated to Congress by the Constitution. Try to find such a delegation! The Supreme Court holds the act void on this ground. Two-thirds of both houses of Congress re-enact the law over the veto of the Court and it thereby becomes valid and effective. The result is that we have amended the Constitution by delegating a new power to Congress but without giving the states their present power to ratify or reject the change. It is not our present purpose to decide whether or not that is a good thing to do; but we ought to understand clearly that that is just what the proposal involves.

Secondly, these short-cut amendments do not originate as proposals for amendments and are not debated as such. They begin as ordinary statutes and the effect of the overriding action of Congress is to make part of the Constitution the principle of constitutional law embodied in them. A good deal of confusion would be injected into our constitutional law by this method of piecemeal amendment. It would seem to be more satisfactory, if we want Congress to punish those guilty of lynching, to amend the Constitution by the usual process, rather than to put beyond judicial reach a statute passed by Congress and invalidated by the Court. If we need an easier method of constitutional amendment, various ways could be found of getting it. It is doubtful if the present plan would be one of them.

The sponsors of this plan, however, will hardly let the argument rest here. They will emphasize that it is only our judicial tradition, and not inescapable logic, which leads us to assume that the Constitution must mean what the Supreme Court says it means, rather than what Congress says it means. We are not necessarily changing the Constitution in overriding the Court. They point out that Congress has been highly conservative in proposing amendments by a two-thirds vote. It has been possible to muster the two-thirds vote necessary to override the presidential veto very infrequently, and there is every reason to suppose that Congress would treat with great respect any really convincing opinion of the Court invalidating a law. The proposal, in short, would probably be much less revolutionary in operation than it sounds on paper.

Curbing the Court's Power by Constitutional Amendment

Lastly it is proposed that we pass a constitutional amendment which would take away from the Supreme Court (and all the other courts presumably) all power to declare acts of Congress unconstitutional. This plan is simple and thorough. It makes Congress the final judge of its own powers under the Constitution. It is foolish to urge that the country would go to the dogs or to the reds, if this important change were made. No other constitutional government in the world gives to its courts the broad power of judicial review which our Supreme Court enjoys. The British Parliament is sovereign and no English court can declare an act of Parliament unconstitutional. In France there is a written constitution under which the French Parliament functions, but no French court has the power to invalidate any act of Parliament. To say that constitutional government cannot work satisfactorily without judicial review gives the lie to the constitutional experience of all the rest of the world. But that does not mean that the abolition of judicial review would not be a fundamental change in the American system. In passing judgment on the proposal there are a number of things to remember. In our entire history less than eighty acts of Congress have been held void by the Supreme Court, but those seventy odd decisions are no index of the practical effect of the power of judicial review. Our whole law-making system is profoundly influenced by the fact that Congress does not have the last word on constitutional questions. The congressman works in the knowledge that the laws he enacts will sooner or later be passed on by the Court. That may make him conservative, perhaps too conservative, since he may be unwilling to support needed legislation which he believes the Court will invalidate. It often centers legislative debates more sharply on constitutional questions than on issues of general policy. On the other hand, the knowledge that there is an ultimate reviewing power in the Court offers the less scrupulous congressman the chance to build his political fences by supporting popular laws without worrying about their constitutionality. He has the comforting assurance that the Court will invalidate them if they are enacted. He evades his own responsibility to support the Constitution and passes the buck to the Court. Those favoring the abolition of judicial review of acts of Congress would do well to make a realistic appraisal of Congress not only when it is on its best behavior, but when it is in its less inhibited moods. Does it have or can it develop a sense of constitutional responsibility anywhere near approaching that of the British Parliament?

Another fact should be kept in mind. The Supreme Court does not confine itself to invalidating acts dear to the hearts of social and economic reformers. Sometimes it has occasion to hold void laws which invade the constitutional civil rights of the citizen, his freedom of speech, his religious liberty, his equality before the law, his right to a fair trial. If judicial review is abolished these rights also are left to the legislative discretion for their protection. In the Spring of 1936 the writer heard Mr. Norman Thomas declare (and herein he apparently differs from the platform doctrines of the party of which he is a candidate) that we can not afford to lose the protection which judicial review gives to our civil liberties and he was unwilling to advocate the abolition of that power. It is also well to remember that after a century and a half of political experience we have become a very "judicially-minded" people. We have not developed any very deep admiration for our legislative bodies. In fact we accord them much less respect than they deserve. And even the common citizen who feels free to criticize particular Supreme Court decisions which he does not like is going to

feel very insecure when he finds that there is no Supreme Court to which he can appeal against what he believes to be a legislative invasion of his rights and liberties. The extent to which the judicial review of legislation is embedded in our fundamental American tradition and mode of thinking about our government, is a factor which we cannot ignore in evaluating the merits of this present proposal. If we were starting from scratch, undeterred by our long political and judicial experience and our subconscious reliance upon our courts for the protection of our rights we might feel much freer to set up a new constitutional system without judicial review, than we can possibly feel to remove the power of judicial review from a constitutional system which has been dominated by it for so long.

Must the Constitution Be Amended?

4. This brings us to the fourth and final position which may be taken by those who believe that our constitutional and judicial system calls for some change. This position is that we should change our Constitution to meet new demands rather than change the Court. Accepting judicial review as a going concern we can all agree that it is most open to attack where the Supreme Court is interpreting the vague and general clauses of the Constitution or is applying an ancient provision to conditions lying beyond the contemplation of the founding fathers. This is clear from our earlier analysis of the New Deal decisions. Now it is wholly intelligent to suggest that if the results we are getting from judicial review under these circumstances are not satisfactory then the thing to do is to sharpen and clarify the constitutional provisions which the Court has to interpret. Since wise men disagree as to whether the due

process clause forbids the enactment of a minimum wage, a simple solution would be to put into the Constitution a definite grant of authority to fix wages and working conditions. That would take the matter out of the realm of judicial debate and put it where it belongs, in the field of political debate. Are there to be no limits to the amount of "stretching" of the delegated powers of Congress to meet the growing demands of our national life? Must they inevitably be construed to cover all the emerging problems calling for centralized control?

In demanding that the Supreme Court permit the commerce clause, the taxing clause, or other constitutional clauses to serve as constitutional pegs upon which to hang new and drastic regulatory programs penetrating into hitherto unoccupied fields of governmental power we are asking them to exercise very broad discretion. If they refuse to do the necessary stretching we may well consider whether the powers of Congress ought not to be frankly and openly increased rather than stretched. The writer is one of those who finds the dissenting opinions in the A.A.A. and Guffey Act cases much more convincing on constitutional grounds than the opinions of the Court. At the same time if American agriculture and mining demand national regulation there is much to be said for giving to Congress clearly and unmistakably the powers we feel it should have. It will hardly be denied that if Congress ought to have the power to prohibit child labor we should do much better to ratify the pending child-labor amendment than to use the backstairs method of driving child labor out of existence by destructive taxation or by denying the employers of children the privileges of interstate commerce.

The Court now occupies the position of exercising a very broad discretion in drawing the limits of governmental power granted in vague terms and under vague limitations. If we do not like the way it does that job it is quite possible to change the Court's job by defining those powers with some precision and sharpening the terms of the limitations. We might give to Congress, free from all doubt, the powers which it needs in order to deal with the pressing problems of present day national life. The uncertainties of the due process limitation may be met by specific clauses clarifying its application.

It is no adequate objection to this proposal to point out the difficulty of drafting such amendments. It is always difficult to draft constitutional provisions which mean exactly what we wish them to mean — and no more. The difficulty, though great, is not insuperable. To refrain from making such grants of power merely because of the difficulty of phrasing them is to confess either lack of skill in the art of draftsmanship, or our inability to make up our minds what we wish to accomplish. But if we do not really know what new powers we wish to grant we should probably refrain from granting them.

There are many, however, who are skeptical of this proposal. They ask whether we can give Congress enough power to control industry and handle all our truly national problems effectively without destroying the basis of federalism, without virtually destroying the states. This may be met by suggesting that we are merely making a formal transfer from state to nation of powers of economic and social control which by their very nature and scope the states have never exercised and never can. A more serious criticism is that which urges, in the light of the history of the Child

Labor Amendment, that it is politically impossible to secure the adoption of any constitutional amendment affecting vital economic questions. But while argument can be made for an easier method of constitutional amendment, those who favor constitutional change by the present process of amendment will hardly be shaken from their position by being told that the amendments they propose will not be readily adopted.

Conclusion

The New Deal cases emphasize the position of supremacy which the Supreme Court occupies in the American constitutional system. Chief Justice Hughes is doubtless bored by the constant repetition of his epigram "We are under a Constitution, but the Constitution is what the judges say it is." It is a practical man's appraisal of the realities of the constitutional system under which we live. This judicial supremacy has arisen in part from the very nature of the judicial process of interpreting and applying the law, and it has been increased by the vagueness and generality of the constitutional clauses which have to be construed.

If we are satisfied with the present system and its results we will naturally have no proposals to make. If we feel that the constitutional wreckage left by the New Deal decisions is due to the abuse of judicial power rather than to the inadequacy of the Constitution to modern needs, then we may logically demand some limitation on the power of the Supreme Court. We shall in this case need to be cautious to see that we do not create more problems than we solve. We may, however, feel that our present difficulties are due partly to an over-zealous extension of judicial power and partly to the failure of an 18th century Constitution to meet adequately the demands of the 20th century. In this case we may attempt to solve both problems by clarifying amendments to the Constitution. This will not only modernize the Constitution, but it will also narrow the field of judicial review by sharpening the vague clauses of the Constitution under which the Supreme Court is now engaged, almost of necessity, in the work of national policy determination.

This plan might well be tried before anything is "done to" the Court, since it promises not only an immediate adjustment of the Constitution to the current of our present national life, but also a forced retirement of the Court from the fields of constitutional construction in which it faces the greatest difficulty and incurs the sharpest criticism.

REORGANIZATION OF THE FEDERAL JUDICIARY

Mr. King, from the Committee on the Judiciary, submitted the following:

Adverse Report
(To accompany S. 1392)

THE Committee on the Judiciary, to whom was referred the bill (S. 1392) to reorganize the judicial branch of the Government after full consideration, having unanimously amended the measure, hereby report the bill adversely with the recommendation that it do not pass. . . .

The committee recommends that the measure be rejected for the following primary reasons:

I. The bill does not accomplish any one of the objectives for which it was originally offered.

II. It applies force to the judiciary and in its initial and ultimate effect would undermine the independence of the courts.

III. It violates all precedents in the history of our Government and would in itself be a dangerous precedent for the future.

IV. The theory of the bill is in direct violation of the spirit of the American Constitution and its employment would permit alteration of the Constitution without the people's consent or approval; it undermines the protection our constitutional system gives to minorities and is subversive of the rights of individuals.

V. It tends to centralize the Federal district judiciary by the power of assigning judges from one district to another at will.

VI. It tends to expand political control over the judicial department by adding to the powers of the legislative and executive departments respecting the judiciary.

This measure was sent to the Congress by the President on Feb. 5, 1937, with a message (appendix A) setting forth the objectives sought to be attained.

It should be pointed out here that a substantial portion of the message was devoted to a discussion of the evils of conflicting decisions by inferior courts on constitutional questions and to the alleged abuse of the power of injunction by some of the Federal courts. These matters, however, have no bearing on the bill before us, for it contains neither a line nor a sentence dealing with either of those problems.

Nothing in this measure attempts to control, regulate, or prohibit the power of any Federal court to pass upon the constitutionality of any law — State or National.

Nothing in this measure attempts to control, regulate, or prohibit the issuance of injunctions by any court, in any case, whether or not the Government is a party to it.

If it were to be conceded that there is need of reform in these respects, it must be understood that this bill does not deal with these problems. . . .

It thus appears that the bill before us does not with certainty provide for in-

Senate Reports on Public Bills, Etc., I (January 5–August 21, 1937), 75 Congress, 1 session, Report No. 711, Calendar No. 734.

creasing the personnel of the Federal judiciary, does not remedy the law's delay, does not serve the interest of the "poorer litigant" and does not provide for the "constant" or "persistent infusion of new blood" into the judiciary. What, then, does it do?

The answer is clear. It applies force to the judiciary. It is an attempt to impose upon the courts a course of action, a line of decision which, without that force, without that imposition, the judiciary might not adopt.

Can there be any doubt that this is the purpose of the bill? Increasing the personnel is not the object of this measure; infusing young blood is not the object; for if either one of these purposes had been in the minds of the proponents, the drafters would not have written the following clause to be found on page 2, lines 1 to 4, inclusive:

"*Provided,* That no additional judge shall be appointed hereunder if the judge who is of retirement age dies, resigns, or retires prior to the nomination of such additional judge."

Let it also be borne in mind that the President's message submitting this measure contains the following sentence:

"If, on the other hand, any judge eligible for retirement should feel that his court would suffer because of an increase of its membership, he may retire or resign under already existing provisions of law if he wishes to do so."

Moreover, the Attorney General in testifying before the committee (hearings, pt. 1, p. 33) said:

"If the Supreme Court feels that the addition of six judges would be harmful to that Court, it can avoid that result by resigning."

Three invitations to the members of the Supreme Court over 70 years of age to get out despite all the talk about

increasing personnel to expedite the disposition of cases and remedy the law's delay. One by the bill. One by the President's message. One by the Attorney General.

Can reasonable men by any possibility differ about the constitutional impropriety of such a course?

Those of us who hold office in this Government, however humble or exalted it may be, are creatures of the Constitution. To it we owe all the power and authority we possess. Outside of it we have none. We are bound by it in every official act.

We know that this instrument, without which we would not be able to call ourselves presidents, judges, or legislators, was carefully planned and deliberately framed to establish three coordinate branches of government, every one of them to be independent of the others. For the protection of the people, for the preservation of the rights of the individual, for the maintenance of the liberties of minorities, for maintaining the checks and balances of our dual system, the three branches of the Government were so constituted that the independent expression of honest difference of opinion could never be restrained in the people's servants and no one branch could overawe or subjugate the others. That is the American system. It is immeasurably more important, immeasurably more sacred to the people of America, indeed, to the people of all the world, than the immediate adoption of any legislation, however beneficial.

That judges should hold office during good behavior is the prescription. It is founded upon historic experience of the utmost significance. Compensation at stated times, which compensation was not to be diminished during their tenure, was also ordained. Those comprehensible terms were the outgrowths of experience which was deep-seated. Of the 55 men in the Constitutional Convention, nearly one-half had actually fought in the War for Independence. Eight of the men present had signed the Declaration of Independence, in which, giving their reasons for the act, they had said of their king: "He has made judges dependent upon his will alone for their tenure of office and the amount and payment of their salaries." They sought to correct an abuse and to prevent its recurrence. When these men wrote the Constitution of their new Government, they still sought to avoid such an abuse as had led to such a bloody war as the one through which they had just passed. So they created a judicial branch of government consisting of courts not conditionally but absolutely independent in the discharge of their functions, and they intended that entire and impartial independence should prevail. Interference with this independence was prohibited, not partially but totally. Behavior other than good was the sole and only cause for interference. This judicial system is the priceless heritage of every American.

By this bill another and wholly different cause is proposed for the intervention of executive influence, namely, age. Age and behavior have no connection; they are unrelated subjects. By this bill, judges who have reached 70 years of age may remain on the bench and have their judgment augmented if they agree with the new appointee, or vetoed if they disagree. This is far from the independence intended for the courts by the framers of the Constitution. This is an unwarranted influence accorded the appointing agency, contrary to the spirit of the Constitution. The bill sets up a plan which has as its stability the changing will or inclination of an agency not a part of the judicial system. Constitutionally, the bill can have no sanction. The effect of the bill, as stated by the Attorney General to the committee, and indeed by the President in both his message and speech, is in violation of the organic law.

No amount of sophistry can cover up this fact. The effect of this bill is not to provide for an increase in the number of Justices composing the Supreme Court. The effect is to provide a forced retirement or, failing in this, to take from the Justices affected a free exercise of their independent judgment.

The President tells us in his address to the Nation of March 9 (appendix D), Congressional Record, March 10, page 2650:

"When the Congress has sought to stabilize national agriculture, to improve the conditions of labor, to safeguard business against unfair competition, to protect our national resources, and in many other ways, to serve our clearly national needs, the majority of the Court has been assuming the power to pass on the wisdom of these acts of the Congress and to approve or disapprove the public policy written into these laws. . . .

"We have, therefore, reached the point as a nation where we must take action to save the Constitution from the Court and the Court from itself. We must find a way to take an appeal from the Supreme Court to the Constitution itself. We want a Supreme Court which will do justice under the Constitution — not over it. In our courts we want a government of laws and not of men."

These words constitute a charge that the Supreme Court has exceeded the boundaries of its jurisdiction and invaded the field reserved by the Constitution to the legislative branch of the Government. At best the accusation is opinion only. It is not the conclusion of judicial process.

Here is the frank acknowledgement

that neither speed nor "new blood" in the judiciary is the object of this legislation, but a change in the decisions of the Court — a subordination of the views of the judges to the views of the executive and legislative, a change to be brought about by forcing certain judges off the bench or increasing their number.

Let us, for the purpose of the argument, grant that the Court has been wrong, wrong not only in that it has rendered mistaken opinions but wrong in the far more serious sense that it has substituted its will for the congressional will in the matter of legislation. May we nevertheless safely punish the Court?

Today it may be the Court which is charged with forgetting its constitutional duties. Tomorrow it may be the Congress. The next day it may be the Executive. If we yield to temptation now to lay the lash upon the Court, we are only teaching others how to apply it to ourselves and to the people when the occasion seems to warrant. Manifestly, if we may force the hand of the Court to secure our interpretation of the Constitution, then some succeeding Congress may repeat the process to secure another and a different interpretation and one which may not sound so pleasant in our ears as that for which we now contend.

There is a remedy for usurpation or other judicial wrongdoing. If this bill be supported by the toilers of this country upon the ground that they want a Court which will sustain legislation limiting hours and providing minimum wages, they must remember that the procedure employed in the bill could be used in another administration to lengthen hours and to decrease wages. If farmers want agricultural relief and favor this bill upon the ground that it gives them a Court which will sustain legislation in their favor, they must remember that the pro-

cedure employed might some day be used to deprive them of every vestige of a farm relief.

When members of the Court usurp legislative powers or attempt to exercise political power, they lay themselves open to the charge of having lapsed from that "good behavior" which determines the period of their official life. But, if you say, the process of impeachment is difficult and uncertain, the answer is, the people made it so when they framed the Constitution. It is not for us, the servants of the people, the instruments of the Constitution, to find a more easy way to do that which our masters made difficult.

But, if the fault of the judges is not so grievous as to warrant impeachment, if their offense is merely that they have grown old, and we feel, therefore, that there should be a "constant infusion of new blood," then obviously the way to achieve that result is by constitutional amendment fixing definite terms for the members of the judiciary or making mandatory their retirement at a given age. Such a provision would indeed provide for the constant infusion of new blood, not only now but at all times in the future. The plan before us is but a temporary expedient which operates once and then never again, leaving the Court as permanently expanded to become once more a court of old men, gradually year by year falling behind the times.

How much better to proceed according to the rule laid down by the Constitution itself than by indirection to achieve our purposes. The futility and absurdity of the devious rather than the direct method is illustrated by the effect upon the problem of the retirement of Justice Van Devanter. . . .

But, if you say the process of reform by amendment is difficult and uncertain, the answer is, the people made it so when they framed the Constitution, and it is not for us, the servants of the people, by indirection to evade their will, or by devious methods to secure reforms upon which they only in their popular capacity have the right to pass.

This bill is an invasion of judicial power such as has never before been attempted in this country. It is true that in the closing days of the administration of John Adams a bill was passed creating 16 new circuit judges while reducing by one the number of places on the Supreme Court. It was charged that this was a bill to use the judiciary for a political purpose by providing official positions for members of a defeated party. The repeal of that law was the first task of the Jefferson administration.

Neither the original act nor the repealer was an attempt to change the course of judicial decision. And never in the history of the country has there been such an act. The present bill comes to us, therefore, wholly without precedent.

It is true that the size of the Supreme Court has been changed from time to time, but in every instance after the Adams administration, save one, the changes were made for purely administrative purposes in aid of the Court, not to control it.

Because the argument has been offered that these changes justify the present proposal, it is important to review all of the instances.

They were seven in number.

The first was by the act of 1801 reducing the number of members from six, as originally constituted, to five. Under the Judiciary Act of 1789 the circuit courts were trial courts and the Justices of the Supreme Court sat in them. That onerous duty was removed by the act of 1801 which created new judgeships for the purpose of relieving the members of

the Supreme Court of this task. Since the work of the Justices was thereby reduced, it was provided that the next vacancy should not be filled. Jeffersonians explained the provision by saying that it was intended merely to prevent Jefferson from making an appointment of a successor to Justice Cushing, whose death was expected.

The next change was in 1802 when the Jefferson administration restored the membership to six.

In neither of these cases was the purpose to influence decisions.

The third change was in 1807 under Jefferson when three new States having been admitted to the Union, a new judicial circuit had to be created, and since it would be impossible for any of the six sitting Justices of the Supreme Court to undertake the trial work in the new circuit (Ohio, Kentucky, and Tennessee), a seventh Justice was added because of the expansion of the country. Had Jefferson wanted to subjugate John Marshall this was his opportunity to multiply members of the Court and overwhelm him, but he did not do it. We have no precedent here.

Thirty years elapsed before the next change. The country had continued to expand. New States were coming in and the same considerations which caused the increase of 1807 moved the representatives of the new West in Congress to demand another expansion. In 1826 a bill adding three justices passed both Houses but did not survive the conference. Andrew Jackson, who was familiar with the needs of the new frontier States, several times urged the legislation. Finally it was achieved in 1837 and the Court was increased from 7 to 9 members.

Here again the sole reason for the change was the need of a growing country for a larger Court. We are still without a precedent.

In 1863 the western frontiers had reached the Pacific. California had been a State since 1850 without representation on the Supreme Court. The exigencies of the war and the development of the coast region finally brought the fifth change when by the act of 1863 a Pacific circuit was created and consequently a tenth member of the High Court.

The course of judicial opinion had not the slightest bearing upon the change.

Seventy-five years of constitutional history and still no precedent for a legislative attack upon the judicial power.

Now we come to the dark days of the reconstruction era for the sixth and seventh alterations of the number of justices.

The congressional majority in Andrew Johnson's administration had slight regard for the rights of minorities and no confidence in the President. Accordingly, a law was passed in 1866, providing that no appointments should be made to the Court until its membership had been reduced from 10 to 7. Doubtless, Thaddeus Stevens feared that the appointees of President Johnson might not agree with reconstruction policies and, if a constitutional question should arise, might vote to hold unconstitutional an act of Congress. But whatever the motive, a reduction of members at the instance of the bitterest majority that ever held sway in Congress to prevent a President from influencing the Court is scarcely a precedent for the expansion of the Court now.

By the time General Grant had become President, in March, 1869, the Court had been reduced to 8 members by the operation of the law of 1866. Presidential appointments were no longer resented, so Congress passed a new law, this time fixing the membership at 9. This law was passed in April, 1869, an important date

to remember, for the legal tender decision had not yet been rendered. Grant was authorized to make the additional appointment in December. Before he could make it, however, Justice Grier resigned, and there were thus two vacancies.

The charge has been made that by the appointment to fill these vacancies Grant packed the Court to affect its decision in the legal tender case. Now whatever Grant's purpose may have been in making the particular appointments, it is obvious that Congress did not create the vacancies for the purpose of affecting any decision, because the law was passed long before the Court had acted in Hepburn v. Griswold and Congress made only one vacancy, but two appointments were necessary to change the opinion.

It was on Feb. 7, 1870, that the Court handed down its judgment holding the Legal Tender Act invalid, a decision very much deplored by the administration. It was on the same date that Grant sent down the nomination of the two justices whose votes, on a reconsideration of the issue, caused a reversal of the decision. As it happens, Grant had made two other nominations first, that of his Attorney General, Ebenezer Hoar, who was rejected by the Senate, and Edwin Stanton, who died four days after having been confirmed. These appointments were made in December, 1869, two months before the decision, and Stanton was named, according to Charles Warren, historian of the Supreme Court, not because Grant wanted him but because a large majority of the members of the Senate and the House urged it. So Grant must be acquitted of having packed the Court and Congress is still without a precedent for any act that will tend to impair the independence of the Court.

Shall we now, after 150 years of loyalty to the constitutional ideal of an untrammeled judiciary, duty bound to protect the constitutional rights of the humblest citizen even against the Government itself, create the vicious precedent which must necessarily undermine our system? The only argument for the increase which survives analysis is that Congress should enlarge the Court so as to make the policies of this administration effective.

We are told that a reactionary oligarchy defies the will of the majority, that this is a bill to "unpack" the Court, and give effect to the desires of the majority; that is to say a bill to increase the number of Justices for the express purpose of neutralizing the views of some of the present members. In justification we are told, but without authority, by those who would rationalize this program, that Congress was given the power to determine the size of the Court so that the legislative branch would be able to impose its will upon the judiciary. This amounts to nothing more than the declaration that when the Court stands in the way of a legislative enactment, the Congress may reverse the ruling by enlarging the Court. When such a principle is adopted, our constitutional system is overthrown!

This, then, is the dangerous precedent we are asked to establish. When proponents of the bill assert, as they have done, that Congress in the past has altered the number of Justices upon the Supreme Court and that this is reason enough for our doing it now, they show how important precedents are and prove that we should now refrain from any action that would seem to establish one which could be followed hereafter whenever a Congress and an executive should become dissatisfied with the decisions of the Supreme Court.

This is the first time in the history of our country that a proposal to alter the decisions of the Court by enlarging its personnel has been so boldly made. Let us meet it. Let us now set a salutary precedent that will never be violated. Let us, of the Seventy-fifth Congress, in words that will never be disregarded by any succeeding Congress, declare that we would rather have an independent Court, a fearless Court, a Court that will dare to announce its honest opinions in what it believes to be the defense of the liberties of the people, than a Court that, out of fear or sense of obligation to the appointing power, or factional passion, approves any measure we may enact. We are not the judges of the judges. We are not above the Constitution.

Even if every charge brought against the so-called "reactionary" members of this Court be true, it is far better that we await orderly but inevitable change of personnel than that we impatiently overwhelm them with new members. Exhibiting this restraint, thus demonstrating our faith in the American system, we shall set an example that will protect the independent American judiciary from attack as long as this Government stands.

It is essential to the continuance of our constitutional democracy that the judiciary be completely independent of both the executive and legislative branches of the Government, and we assert that independent courts are the last safeguard of the citizen, where his rights, reserved to him by the express and implied provisions of the Constitution, come in conflict with the power of governmental agencies. We assert that the language of John Marshall, then in his seventy-sixth year, in the Virginia Convention (1829–31), was and is prophetic:

"Advert, sir, to the duties of a judge. He has to pass between the Government and the man whom the Government is prosecuting; between the most powerful individual in the community and the poorest and most unpopular. It is of the last importance that in the exercise of these duties he should observe the utmost fairness. Need I express the necessity of this? Does not every man feel that his own personal security and the security of his property depends on that fairness? The judicial department comes home in its effect to every man's fireside; it passes on his property, his reputation, his life, his all. Is it not, to the last degree, important that he should be rendered perfectly and completely independent, with nothing to influence or control him but God and his conscience?". . .

The whole bill prophesies and permits executive and legislative interferences with the independence of the Court, a prophecy and a permission which constitute an affront to the spirit of the Constitution.

"The complete independence of the courts of justice is peculiarly essential in a limited Constitution. By a limited Constitution, I understand one which contains certain specified exceptions to the legislative authority; such, for instance, as that it shall pass no bills of attainder, no ex-post-facto laws, and the like. Limitations of this kind can be preserved in practice no other way than through the medium of courts of justice, whose duty it must be to declare all acts contrary to the manifest tenor of the Constitution void. Without this, all the reservations of particular rights or privileges would amount to nothing." (The Federalist, vol. 2, p. 100, no. 78.)

The spirit of the Constitution emphasizing the establishment of an independent judicial branch was re-enunciated by Madison in Nos. 47 and 48 (The Federalist, vol. 1, pp. 329, 339) and by John Adams (Adams' Works, vol. 1, p. 186).

If interference with the judgment of an independent judiciary is to be countenanced in any degree, then it is permitted and sanctioned in all degrees. There is no constituted power to say where the degree ends or begins, and the political administration of the hour may apply the essential "concepts of justice" by equipping the courts with one strain of "new blood," while the political administration of another day use a different light and a different blood test. Thus would influence run riot. Thus perpetuity, independence, and stability belonging to the judicial arm of the Government and relied on by lawyers and laity, are lost. Thus is confidence extinguished.

From the very beginning of our Government to this hour, the fundamental necessity of maintaining inviolate the independencce of the three coordinate branches of government has been recognized by legislators, jurists, and presidents. . . .

In other words, the framers of the Constitution were not satisfied to give the Court power to pass only on cases arising under the laws but insisted on making it quite clear that the power extends to cases arising "under the Constitution." Moreover, Article VI of the Constitution, clause 2, provides:

"This Constitution and the laws of the United States which shall be made in pursuance thereof . . . shall be the supreme law of the land. . . ."

Language was never more clear. No doubt can remain. A pretended law which is not "in pursuance" of the Constitution is no law at all.

A citizen has the right to appeal to the Constitution from such a statute. He has the right to demand that Congress shall not pass any act in violation of that instrument, and, if Congress does pass such an act, he has the right to seek refuge in the courts and to expect the Supreme Court to strike down the act if it does in fact violate the Constitution. A written constitution would be valueless if it were otherwise.

The right and duty of the Court to construe the Constitution is thus made clear. The question may, however, be propounded whether in construing that instrument the Court has undertaken to "override the judgment of the Congress on legislative policy." It is not necessary for this committee to defend the Court from such a charge. An invasion of the legislative power by the judiciary would not, as has already been indicated, justify the invasion of judicial authority by the legislative power. The proper remedy against such an invasion is provided in the Constitution.

We may, however, point out that neither in this administration nor in any previous administration has the Supreme Court held unconstitutional more than a minor fraction of the laws which have been enacted. In 148 years, from 1789 to 1937, only sixty-four acts of Congress have been declared unconstitutional — sixty-four acts out of a total of approximately 58,000. . . .

These 64 acts were held invalid in 76 cases, 30 of which were decided by the unanimous vote of all the justices, 9 by the agreement of all but one of the justices, 14 by the agreement of all but two, another 12 by agreement of all but three. In 11 cases only were there as many as four dissenting votes when the laws were struck down.

Only four statutes enacted by the present administration have been declared unconstitutional with three or more dissenting votes. And only eleven statutes, or parts thereof, bearing approval of the present Chief Executive out of 2,669 signed by him during his first adminis-

tration, have been invalidated. Of the eleven, three — the Municipal Bankruptcy Act, the Farm Mortgage Act and the Railroad Pension Act — were not what have been commonly denominated administration measures. When he attached his signature to the Railroad Pension Act, the President was quoted as having expressed his personal doubt as to the constitutionality of the measure. The Farm Mortgage Act was later rewritten by the Congress, reenacted, and in its new form sustained by the Court which had previously held it void. Both the Farm Mortgage Act in its original form and the National Recovery Administration Act were held to be unconstitutional by a unanimous vote of all the justices. With this record of fact, it can scarcely be said with accuracy that the legislative power has suffered seriously at the hands of the Court.

But even if the case were far worse than it is alleged to be, it would still be no argument in favor of this bill to say that the courts and some judges have abused their power. The courts are not perfect, nor are the judges. The Congress is not perfect, nor are Senators and Representatives. The Executive is not perfect. These branches of government and the offices under them are filled by human beings who for the most part strive to live up to the dignity and idealism of a system that was designed to achieve the greatest possible measure of justice and freedom for all the people. We shall destroy the system when we reduce it to the imperfect standards of the men who operate it. We shall strengthen it and ourselves, we shall make justice and liberty for all men more certain when, by patience and self-restraint, we maintain it on the high plane on which it was conceived.

Inconvenience and even delay in the

enactment of legislation is not a heavy price to pay for our system. Constitutional democracy moves forward with certainty rather than with speed. The safety and the permanence of the progressive march of our civilization are far more important to us and to those who are to come after us than the enactment now of any particular law. The Constitution of the United States provides ample opportunity for the expression of popular will to bring about such reforms and changes as the people may deem essential to their present and future welfare. It is the people's charter of the powers granted those who govern them. . . .

We recommend the rejection of this bill as a needless, futile, and utterly dangerous abandonment of constitutional principle.

It was presented to the Congress in a most intricate form and for reasons that obscured its real purpose.

It would not banish age from the bench nor abolish divided decisions.

It would not affect the power of any court to hold laws unconstitutional nor withdraw from any judge the authority to issue injunctions.

It would not reduce the expense of litigation nor speed the decision of cases.

It is a proposal without precedent and without justification.

It would subjugate the courts to the will of Congress and the President and thereby destroy the independence of the judiciary, the only certain shield of individual rights.

It contains the germ of a system of centralized administration of law that would enable an executive so minded to send his judges into every judicial district in the land to sit in judgment on controversies between the Government and the citizen.

It points the way to the evasion of the Constitution and establishes the method whereby the people may be deprived of their right to pass upon all amendments of the fundamental law.

It stands now before the country, acknowledged by its proponents as a plan to force judicial interpretation of the Constitution, a proposal that violates every sacred tradition of American democracy.

Under the form of the Constitution it seeks to do that which is unconstitutional.

Its ultimate operation would be to make this Government one of men rather than one of law, and its practical operation would be to make the Constitution what the executive or legislative branches of the Government choose to say it is — an interpretation to be changed with each change of administration.

It is a measure which should be so emphatically rejected that its parallel will never again be presented to the free representatives of the free people of America.

EXCERPTS FROM SENATE DEBATE

SENATOR JOSEPH T. ROBINSON

Mr. President, those who have collaborated in the preparation of the substitute amendment, particularly including the Senator from Kentucky (Mr. Logan), the Senator from New Mexico (Mr. Hatch), and myself, have had in mind the criticisms which have been directed in public addresses, and in news and magazine articles, against the original bill, presented by the Senator from Arizona (Mr. Ashurst), the chairman of the Committee on the Judiciary, very shortly after the President sent to the Congress his message on this important subject.

As everyone who hears me realizes, there has been great diversity of opinion not only among those who are opposed to any legislation providing for the reorganization of the Federal courts, but also among those who feel that conditions justify, if they do not require, a change in our statutes relating to the questions at issue.

The Substitute

The substitute amendment provides for the appointment of one Justice in each calendar year in relation to such Justices of the Supreme Court as may be serving after they have reached the age of 75 years. There seems to be widespread if not general or universal sentiment in favor of the retirement of Justices who have attained that age. It is not that all men who reach 75 lose their powers of reasoning or of judgment, but it is that by common acceptance those who have passed beyond 75 usually are in a state of mental and physical decline. Our statutes have recognized the wisdom and the necessity for judges who have the physical vigor to perform the tasks that are assigned to them. Heretofore provision has been made for voluntary retirement at the age of 70 years, and that policy has not only been approved in general public opinion but it has been advocated by some Justices of the Supreme Court who now have passed far beyond 70 years, and who quite naturally are unable to apply to themselves the theory and the doctrine they have sought to apply to other judges.

The statute, as proposed in the pending amendment in the nature of a substitute, permits the appointment by the President of one additional Justice of the Supreme Court in each calendar year where a Justice or Justices are serving beyond the age of 75. I know it has been said by some, and I expect that it will be repeated in the memorable debate that is to follow my statement, that the principle incorporated in this legislation in the particular to which I am now referring is erroneous, that it is disregardful of the spirit of the Federal Constitution, that it tends to give to the President dictatorial powers. Later, during the course of the debate, it may be my privilege to elaborate the arguments which appear to me consistently to refute that contention. It suffices for my purpose on this occasion to say that during the course of this prolonged controversy Senators who lead the opposition to any legislation have introduced constitutional amendments sub-

Congressional Record, 75 Congress, 1 session, Vol. 81, pp. 6789–6794, 6873–6877, 6966–6967, 6973–6974, 7038–7039, and 7045–7047.

stantially conforming to the provisions of this bill.

No moral or legal reason can be assigned in justification to resorting to the complicated and difficult process of constitutional amendment in preference to the legislative process if it appears that the legislative proposal is itself within the Constitution. I make the declaration now, in order that it may be considered by those who oppose the position I take, that no serious question has been raised by any lawyer, either in this body or in the country at large, that it is within the power of the Congress to enact the legislation contemplated in the proposed substitute; and, if that be true, then the only question left in that particular is one of policy. Manifestly it is neither necessary nor desirable to resort to the slow and difficult process of amending the Constitution if substantially the same ends may be brought about by the enactment of legislation. . . .

MR. AUSTIN. Mr. President, will the Senator yield?

MR. ROBINSON. I yield to the Senator from Vermont.

MR. AUSTIN. My question is this: Does not the Senator from Arkansas consider it just as bad, from a legal point of view and from a moral point of view, if the bill by natural effect and consequence terminates the tenure of office at a point less than for life, as it would if it contained a complete and express statement of a tenure that was less than life, fixed by an act of Congress and not by an amendment to the Constitution?

MR. ROBINSON. The Senator's question answers itself. No lawyer would say that Congress has the power to limit the tenure of a Justice of the Supreme Court to less than life and good behavior, and therefore, no proposal of that nature is presented. But there is, and there has

been for more than 50 years, a feeling in the country among those who constitute its citizenship that men are not always conscious of the time when they have passed the climax of their usefulness. It is well illustrated in politics. One who has served long and well is seldom, if ever, conscious of his failing powers, and he keeps on running for office, running and running and running, until everyone gets tired of him and until some man whom he considers his inferior defeats him for office. (Laughter.)

MR. BURKE and MR. MINTON addressed the Chair.

MR. ROBINSON. I have often thought that politics is not an occupation; it is a disease (laughter); and, by the Eternal, when it gets in the blood and brain, there is no cure for it. (Laughter.)

MR. LEWIS. Mr. President ——

MR. ROBINSON. Just a moment. I have seen dozens of men, discredited and rejected by their constituents, sit on the fence and in the exercise of their "imaginatory" powers — I quote now the Senator from Vermont — see strange hands beckoning them out of the darkness and hear mysterious voices calling them back to run for office again. . . .

MR. ROBINSON. I yield now, first, to the Senator from Indiana.

MR. MINTON. In connection with the proposition the Senator is so ably discussing, I suppose he would accept a statement from very high authority on that point, namely, the present Chief Justice of the United States. In 1928 Chief Justice Hughes said:

Some judges have stayed too long on the bench. It is extraordinary how reluctant aged judges are to retire and to give up their accustomed work. I agree that the importance in the Supreme Court of avoiding the risk of having judges who are unable properly to do their work and yet insist on remaining on the bench is too great to permit chances to be taken, and any age selected must be somewhat arbitrary, as the time of the failing in mental power differs widely.

Mr. ROBINSON. My favorite authority on that subject is not Mr. Chief Justice Hughes; it is Mr. Justice McReynolds.

Mr. MINTON. If the Senator will permit me, I will also quote what Mr. Justice McReynolds said.

Mr. ROBINSON. I myself am going to read that. The Senator could probably make this speech much more effectively than I can make it, but I still maintain that, as a Senator, I have some right to talk a little within my own time.

In October 1914, when the Associate Justice, Mr. McReynolds, was Attorney General, he submitted a report which no doubt is in the mind and memory of my good friend the Senator from Indiana (Mr. Minton). In the performance of his duties he sent an urgent recommendation to Congress, and I shall now read it:

Judges of the United States courts, at the age of 70, after having served 10 years, may retire upon full pay. In the past many judges have availed themselves of this privilege. Some, however, have remained upon the bench long beyond the time they are adequately able to discharge their duties, and in consequence the administration of justice has suffered. I suggest an act —

Not a constitutional amendment, I remind the Senator from Nebraska (Mr. Burke); just an act —

I suggest an act providing that when any judge of a Federal court below the Supreme Court fails to avail himself of the privilege of retiring now granted by law, that the President be required, with the advice and consent of the Senate, to appoint another judge

who would preside over the affairs of the court and have precedence over the older one. This will insure at all times the presence of a judge sufficiently active to discharge promptly and adequately the duties of the court.

It is true that Mr. Justice McReynolds, then Attorney General, limited his recommendation to the inferior courts, the circuit and district courts of the United States, but there is no difference in principle if the doctrine be applied to the Supreme Court as well as to the inferior courts.

Mr. MINTON. Mr. President, will the Senator yield further?

Mr. ROBINSON. I yield to the Senator from Indiana.

Mr. MINTON. I may fortify the Senator's splendid argument with another high authority, another Chief Justice of the United States Supreme Court. He did not limit it to the lower courts and he did not put the age at 75. I refer to the late Honorable Chief Justice Taft, who said:

There is no doubt that there are judges at 70 who have ripe judgments, active minds, and much physical vigor, and that they are able to perform their duties in a very satisfactory way. Yet in a majority of cases when men come to be 70 they have lost vigor, their minds are not as active, their senses not as acute, and their willingness to undertake great labor is not so great as in younger men, and as we ought to have in judges who are to perform the enormous task which falls to the lot of Supreme Court Justices. . . .

Mr. BURKE. Mr. President, will the Senator yield further?

Mr. ROBINSON. Certainly.

Mr. BURKE. The Senator has stated his view of the matter, that this is an unlimited power possessed by Congress to make the Court 10 or 15 or 100, if they wish, and for any purpose or motive that may appeal to the Congress. Do I correctly state the Senator's position?

MR. ROBINSON. Yes. I think there is no limitation in the Constitution on the power of the Congress to prescribe the number of Justices that shall compose the Supreme Court. I would not say it is sound policy to exercise that power for a bad motive, but the power exists, and that is sufficient for this argument.

MR. BURKE. The Senator feels that there is no merit whatever in the position of those who take the view that the reason why the framers of the Constitution did not say, "We shall have a Supreme Court of a certain number," was that Congress might be free to give us at any time a Court of a size that could promptly and efficiently do the work of the Court, and that Congress has no power within the spirit of the Constitution to add any members to the Court for any other purpose.

MR. ASHURST. Mr. President ——

MR. ROBINSON. No, Mr. President; I do not make that statement. The Senator knows I declined to pass judgment on the motives which prompted the framers of the Constitution to leave this power in the Congress. It is a very strong argument that the Senator from Nebraska does not question the existence of the power.

I am glad to yield now to the Senator from Arizona.

MR. ASHURST. Mr. President, when the framers of the Constitution came to create the Supreme Court, they did not by mere accident or inadvertence grant to Congress the power to exercise checks against the overreaching of the liberties of the people by the Court. Many, if not most, of the members of the Convention were scholars; some of them had studied law in the Middle Temple in London,

and most, if not all, of the members were familiar with the judicial tyranny which had taken place in England during the troubled period of the Stuarts and other reigns preceding the drafting of the Constitution.

The framers took meticulous care and much pains, scholars and historians as they were, to see to it that the judicial power they granted to the courts should never run so riot as to thwart the will of the American people. Hence, they not only deliberately made Congress the body that should fix the number of the members of the Court, but they even went so far as to deny the Court the right to fix its own jurisdiction, and the question of jurisdiction of that Court is, within certain limitations, subject to the right and power of Congress to change and modify as and when Congress sees fit.

The framers did not permit the Supreme Court to be the judge of the qualifications of its own members. The framers required the Court to depend upon the Congress for appropriations for its expenses; yea, even its own bailiff.

Nothing in all the history of the Constitution making is more clear than that the makers deliberately saw to it that no judicial branch should be set up that would overreach the legislative branch or the executive branch.

The makers were wise enough also to repose in Congress the legislative power and to grant the Court the Judicial power.

I had not intended to interrupt the able speech of the Senator from Arkansas, but whatever may have been said about this proposed legislation, no lawyer in America has ever said that this bill, if it should become the law, would take any judicial power from the Supreme Court of the United States.

If this bill passes, the courts will possess and exercise the same judicial power they had before, and I venture the assertion that if this bill took any judicial power from the Supreme Court of the United States, there would not be 5 votes for it. . . .

MR. ASHURST. I apologize to the Senator for interrupting him.

MR. ROBINSON. No; the Senator must not apologize. He has contributed very effectively to my remarks; but I am prompted by the question of the Senator from Nebraska, and by the answer that has been made to that question by the Senator from Arizona, to say that my judgment is that the justification for this legislation lies in large part in the fact that the Supreme Court, according to members of that body and according to great Members of the Senate, have gone outside the sphere of their jurisdiction, which is to interpret and apply the laws, and have entered the realm exclusively ascribed to the Congress by the Constitution — the realm of defining public policies.

I see before me today great Senators, whose names will go down in history among the immortals, who have made that statement on the floor of the Senate of the United States, and who now apparently have forgotten the position they took in days gone by. In another address, on a different occasion, it is my intention to show some of the instances in which the Court went outside the sphere of judicial interpretation, and literally wrote into the statutes words that Congress did not incorporate in them, and changed and gave unnatural meanings to words which had better have been naturally interpreted.

In doing that I do not say that the Supreme Court acted corruptly, or that its members were conscious of trespassing upon the jurisdiction of the legislative department. I do affirm, and believe myself able to prove to a jury of lawyers, that the Court is responsible for many of the troubles against which we are now legislating, because it gave unnatural and illogical definitions to terms employed by the Congress in enacting legislation.

MR. BURKE. Mr. President, will the Senator yield?

MR. ROBINSON. I yield to the Senator from Nebraska.

MR. BURKE. Even at the risk of making somewhat of a nuisance of myself ——

MR. ROBINSON. Oh, the Senator cannot do that.

MR. BURKE. I am afraid he has already done it.

MR. ROBINSON. The Senator never makes a nuisance of himself. Whenever he is a nuisance, Nature does it for him. (Laughter.)

MR. BURKE. Very well; but, passing that over, I think it is important that at the start we find out as definitely as we can something of the purpose of this bill. As I understand, the Senator now takes the position that because the Supreme Court, in the opinion of some persons and in his own opinion, has at times gone outside its own function, therefore, it is now proper and legitimate for Congress to make over the Court to some extent in order to see that that does not happen again. Is that the point?

MR. ROBINSON. That is not a very bad statement of my position. It is not entirely accurate; but the thought does appeal to me that if the judiciary trespasses on the jurisdiction of the legislative department, and undertakes, in interpreting statutes, to say what is sound or unsound public policy, Congress has the right — yea, it may be the duty of the legislative branch of the Government — to exercise such powers as it possesses to prevent that usurpation of authority; and the Senator from Nebraska and any other Senator may make the most of that admission.

MR. BURKE. Mr. President, if I may ask just one other question ——

MR. ROBINSON. Yes.

MR. BURKE. Will the Senator, in the course of his remarks — I do not ask him to do it now, but in his own good time — explain to us how he can reconcile the statement he has just made with the principle that we have in this country, and desire to maintain, an independent judiciary?

MR. ROBINSON. Why, certainly — certainly. Independence of the judiciary does not involve or imply usurpation by the judiciary. If the Senator cannot see that without an elaboration of the argument, I think I had better appeal to other minds. My theory is that the demand for this legislation arises principally — not entirely, but principally — out of the fact that the judiciary, not only in the Supreme Court but even in the lower courts, have from time to time confused the question of power with the issue of policy. Do you get it? They have decided that the exercise of a power by the Congress is unconstitutional in some instances when they disapproved the public policy involved in the legislation. That is wrong; and the efforts to prevent it have no sensible relation to the independence of the judiciary. The judiciary must be independent in the sphere ascribed to it by the Constitution. It must not be an outlaw in any other sphere. The mere fact that there is no appeal from the Supreme Court of the United States gives that Court no right to violate constitutional limitations imposed by law and by reason on its own authority.

MR. MINTON. Mr. President, will the Senator yield?

MR. ROBINSON. I yield.

MR. MINTON. If the Supreme Court is doing what the Senator says it is doing — and it is, and has done it times out of number — then it is exercising a legislative function.

MR. ROBINSON. Certainly.

MR. MINTON. And if it is exercising a legislative function, there is no place to which to turn for the redress of a legislative function except the legislature.

MR. ROBINSON. The proposition is self-evident. The Senator has stated it better and more accurately than I could state it.

MR. BORAH. Mr. President ——

MR. ROBINSON. I yield to the Senator from Idaho.

MR. BORAH. If the Supreme Court up to the present time has been exercising legislative power, in what respect does this bill prevent it from exercising legislative power in the future?

MR. ROBINSON. There is not any way by which the Congress can prevent a judge from doing the wrong thing; but the theory of the bill is that it will gradually place on the bench those who will respect, as a primary consideration, the limitations on their own authority. I do not ask you to take my word. I will ask you to take the word of the Senator from Idaho himself.

In 1930, I think, the Senator from Idaho arose on this floor and made an eloquent appeal against the confirmation of a great Chief Justice, solely on the theory that that Chief Justice was disposed to decide questions of public policy rather than questions of limitation on the power of the lawmaking body. The Senator from Idaho may take from now until the end of the threatened filibuster to explain his attitude on that occasion; and he was not alone in that attitude. At the same time a dozen other Senators, among them the brightest and the bravest who are opposing this bill, sought to prevent the confirmation of Mr. Chief

Justice Hughes on the theory that Mr. Hughes would lead the Court out of the proper sphere of judicial determination into the realm of legislation. They could not say anything against his character other than that. They could not question his personal integrity, but they fought him to the bitter death; and I cabled back from London, where I had gone on a mission for the Government, my vote in support of Mr. Hughes, because I believed him to be an honest and an able man. The issue was acute; it was tense; it was hard fought, and there was a large vote in the Senate. At one time it was thought doubtful whether he would be confirmed. The opposition rested their argument solely on the ground that he would legislate as a judge. . . .

Mr. BARKLEY. Mr. President, will the Senator yield?

Mr. ROBINSON. I yield.

Mr. BARKLEY. Is it not true that in the able address made on that occasion by the Senator from Idaho, when asked by another Member of the Senate whether he would remedy the situation by amending the Constitution, he replied no, he would amend the Court?

Mr. ROBINSON. Oh, yes. The Senator from Idaho did not then have any sympathy with amending the Constitution, because he said the same old judges would read an erroneous interpretation into any amendment which might be made, so he favored amending the Court. He may take the pending bill as in a sense an "amendment of the Court," if he wishes to do so, but when he makes an argument against it on that ground, I reply to him in his own language — well-considered, forceful, and influential.

Mr. STEIWER. Mr. President, will the Senator yield?

Mr. ROBINSON. I yield.

Mr. STEIWER. If the members of the Court are disposed to indulge in legisla-

tion, that is to say, to assert their views upon policies rather than their views upon law ——

Mr. ROBINSON. Not always; sometimes.

Mr. STEIWER. I say, if that is the case ——

Mr. ROBINSON. Has the Senator any doubt that that has been the case?

Mr. STEIWER. I have no doubt about it in my own mind.

Mr. ROBINSON. I am only searching the Senator's mind.

Mr. STEIWER. If that is the case, is not the logical and proper means of reaching that to object to the confirmation of the nomination of the judge and not merely to change the composition of the Court?

Mr. ROBINSON. I think that is caviling. After a judge is confirmed he is on the bench for life, and there is no opportunity of knowing what he is going to decide except to use the method employed by the Senator from Idaho and the Senator from Virginia, and say, "From what he has done heretofore, from the clients he has represented, from the methods used in other matters, I think he will be unfair to the public, unconsciously unfair to the public."

Of course, if one knows about those things at the time confirmation occurs, and has not confidence in the judge, he would do just what these Senators did in opposing Mr. Justice Hughes. I cannot say that their judgment of Mr. Hughes is confirmed by the history of his actions as the Chief Justice. I have great respect for that able lawyer. I regard him as a learned and conscientious man, and do not wish to be construed as giving endorsement to the arguments which were employed against his confirmation. I voted for his confirmation. . . .

SENATOR JOSEPH F. GUFFEY

Mr. President, as the subject of my remarks is largely historical, and, I hope, noncontroversial, I request that my colleagues do not interrupt me until I shall have concluded.

Mr. President, this is the age of political realism in the United States. The sham battles that enlivened the atmosphere and amused the spectators in the gay days which preceded the economic depression are a thing of the past. If the actors in the political drama are still unaware of that fact, the audience is not.

The time has arrived when something more than lip service is demanded of those who enlist under the banner of progressivism and liberalism. The people of this country are aroused. They are distrustful of leaders who say, "I am for judicial reform, but I dislike the President's method of accomplishing it." "I am for a bill establishing minimum wages and maximum hours, but I disagree with details of the administration's program." "I am for adequate farm-relief legislation and a decent income for farmers, but I disagree with many features of the administration policy." "I am for conservation and social security and all those things, but I think we ought to go slowly in writing them into law."

Mr. President, when a liberal puts the word "but" after his declaration of political faith it is prima-facie evidence either that he secretly believes in the philosophy of reactionary Bourbonism or else he lacks the courage of his own convictions. The test of office holding should no longer be what a man says he believes. The test should be what he actually does and how he votes.

It is not my purpose to warn my colleagues or to criticize their actions. The Democratic Party sits here today in overwhelming power because we went before the people and solemnly pledged ourselves to outlaw economic wrongs and injustices that have been rankling and festering for generations. For the first time in many years political promises were taken to have definite meaning. The voters in last November's election entrusted into our hands the solemn duty of giving legal and concrete form to the social and economic aspirations of the vast majority of American citizens.

This task lies ahead of us today. This task is bound up completely and inextricably in the current effort of the Democratic Party to transform the United States Supreme Court from a superlegislative body that is above and beyond the law into the kind of impartial tribunal for the adjudication of judicial disputes that it was originally intended to be.

It is futile for Senators to sit here legislating on the most vital aspects of social and economic conditions, if they know in their hearts that what is being done may be arbitrarily overturned by a few aged Justices who substitute their "own political predilections" for the Constitution of the country. This game of political blind man's bluff is about over.

There are persons who proclaim their belief in the purposes of the Roosevelt administration and who believe that the Supreme Court sometime ago set itself against the program of that administration, but who at the same time proclaim that it would be morally wrong to do anything about the Court. I frankly cannot understand such a position, whether it be taken by a Senator, a Member of the House of Representatives, or any other citizen.

Today the public expects something more than a mere recital of ideals and aspirations. The outstanding lesson to be learned from the events of the past few years is the fact that liberal and progressive forces of the Nation can write their program into law, if they stand shoulder to shoulder fighting for the principles in which they profess to believe. The people of progressive turn of mind are in the overwhelming majority in the country, and there is no reason why they should be in a minority here in the Congress of the United States.

The essence of democracy is majority rule. The American people, by a plurality never before equaled in our history, indicated that they desired the enactment of a program of social legislation to meet the conditions which exist today.

They did not ask Congress to think up a lot of legal quibbles and sophistries as to why this cannot be done or that cannot be done. They experienced too much of that type of negative statesmanship in the days of the unfortunate Mr. Hoover. What they want now is not someone to tell them why this or that program cannot be enacted but to point out how it can be enacted. The people would like a demonstration of the fact that progressivism in politics means something more than a constant policy of obstruction and frustration.

In undertaking a discussion of President Roosevelt's program for judicial reform, the first thing to strike the attention is the effort being made by those who oppose social reform to paint the Supreme Court as a hallowed institution whose august members, endowed with qualities of mind almost supernatural, have found a way to distill the pure spirit of law free from the impurities and corrupting influence of bias, passion, or prejudice.

This erroneous myth is being nourished with painful and loving care in the hope that it may become implanted for all time to come as a sacred tradition in the consciousness of the American people. As a matter of concrete fact, nothing could be further from the truth. History shows conclusively that throughout most of its existence the Supreme Court has been enmeshed in partisan party politics, that throughout most of its history it has been openly hailed as the last bulwark of reaction, that its members frequently have been appointed for political considerations, and that this spirit of partisan politics has been very rampant in the present Court.

Unquestionably, the Court was conceived originally by the founding fathers as an institution to be composed of men whose outlook and motivations took root in the rich soil of national patriotism and whose zeal was to be directed to the promotion of even-handed justice and to the impartial interpretation of the Constitution. But in actual practice the Court has fallen woefully short of that idea. The very fact of this debate here today is sufficient evidence to prove that the Court has not played the role assigned to it.

If some of my colleagues are inclined to disagree, let me remind them that the most severe criticisms of the course pursued by the supreme tribunal have come from Senators who are now actively and heatedly opposing the Chief Executive's program of reform and reorganization.

In all the welter of words and arguments over this issue, let us never lose sight of the fundamental fact that this problem confronts us today because the Supreme Court of the United States has been partisan, prejudiced, and biased in denying workingmen and farmers their fundamental legal rights. That is the real core of the issue, and we may as well state that fact bluntly and boldly. Had the Justices been half as zealous in upholding the rights of the poor and lowly as they have been in protecting the property rights of the wealthy, this problem would not be resting on the doorstep of the President and Congress. . . .

In fact, it is accurate and fair to state that the present period of the Supreme Court will go down in history as a time in which partisan politics played a role of great magnitude both in the Court's deliberations and in its decisions.

At this point I think it wise to point out that the foundations for a political court were deliberately laid by the Republican Party elders who ruled this country in the decade following the World War. For proof of that statement, it is necessary only to refer again to the letter written in 1920 by the late President William Howard Taft, and which was first made public in a radio address by our majority leader, the Senator from Arkansas (Mr. Robinson), a few weeks ago. Said Mr. Taft, in explaining why he was supporting the Republican candidate for President:

Take, for instance, the four places likely to be filled by Wilson's successor on the Supreme Court. Think of the danger of another Brandeis and Clark. The power and the usefulness of that Court would be broken down under such appointments if the majority of the Court were to be made up of them.

Mr. Taft stated the case as baldly as it could be stated. Unless the Court was packed with reactionaries who were in effect pledged to oppose every enlightened economic and social step taken by Congress, then the Court, to use his words, would lose its power and influence. It will be noted that Mr. Taft was not concerned for a moment with the legal and constitutional aspects of such a question.

What happened? The Republican candidate, Mr. Harding, was elected and the Court was soundly and solidly packed by him to such an extent that legislation to protect the farmer and the working-man was doomed almost before it was passed.

That was the situation when Mr. Roosevelt came into office, carrying with him a mandate from the mass of American people to reestablish the principle of equal justice under majority rule. That is the condition which has existed almost to this hour. Until the last couple of months, the supreme political power in this country has been the Supreme Court of the United States, and its grip has been broken only by the courage and the single-minded purpose of President Franklin D. Roosevelt.

It is all very well for my colleagues to work themselves into a fury of indignation over Mr. Roosevelt's proposal to enlarge the Supreme Court. It is their privilege to view with alarm and to thunder from the mountain top that the stricken Republic will totter to its doom if any reorganization plan is enacted into law. It is their privilege to picture this issue as a struggle on their part to preserve unsullied and unharmed the springs and sources of judicial power. But I venture to predict that their naive view will find little support when the story of this era is written into history.

The men and women who look at this controversy with the proper degree of detachment will see this struggle for what it is — a contest for political power between two opposing groups whose political philosophies are diametrically opposed. Any man who contends that the Supreme Court itself has not indulged in politics in the last few months is either totally ignorant of what has happened or he has a childlike faith in human nature that is wholly out of place in the realistic sphere of public affairs.

The record now shows positively that until a few months ago a majority of the members of the Supreme Court of the

United States were engaged in the dubious business of blocking the social-reform program of the Roosevelt administration.

We have already seen how the appointment of reactionary judges was a cardinal doctrine in the program of Republican leaders. We can trace the subsequent decisions of these judges on the bench, and we find that in almost every case their so-called judicial opinions were identical with their views on current political questions. In fact, the similarity is too glaring to pass for coincidence. . . .

The resignation of Mr. Justice Van Devanter, coming as it did on the morning when the Senate Judiciary Committee was voting on the reorganization bill, was especially well timed. The country, in fact, has enjoyed the spectacle of the political battling between the respective leaders.

But the people of the United States have a different way of looking at these things. They know an about face when they observe one, and they are sensible enough to know why such things happen. Facts are more impressive to the public than oratory.

It was a glorious day of triumph for the working people of this country when that odious decision of the Supreme Court forbidding the enactment of State minimum-wage laws for women was swept aside; and let me say that the man responsible for that great humane victory, singly and alone is President Franklin D. Roosevelt. . . .

SENATOR BURTON K. WHEELER

. . . When the bill was first introduced the Attorney General of the United States in a radio speech used this language:

Ladies and gentlemen, only 9 short days have passed since the President sent to the Congress recommendations for the reorganization of the Federal judiciary. Yet in that brief time unfriendly voices have filled the air with lamentations and have vexed our ears with insensate clamor calculated to divert attention from the merits of his proposal.

Why was it that immediately there was aroused such feeling that protests came from the masses of the people of the country against the proposal? It was because they felt that the bill was an attempt on the part of the administration to do by indirection what it did not want to do by direction.

Again, Mr. President, after the appeal was made to the drought-stricken farmers in the Dust Bowl that we must immediately pack the Supreme Court in order to afford relief to those farmers, and after an appeal was made to the flood victims along the Ohio River in order to get them stirred up in favor of the proposal and to cause them to send protests to their Senators who were opposed to it, we found another kind of appeal being made. We found an appeal being made by the Postmaster General of the United States on the ground of party loyalty. He contended that every Democrat ought to support the bill because of party loyalty regardless to its effect upon the Constitution of the United States and regardless of its violation of the spirit of the Constitution.

We heard Mr. Farley saying, "It is in the bag." In another place and at another time he said, "We will let the Senate talk and then we will let the House talk. Then we will call the roll. We have the votes." The press of the country after the last election pronounced Mr. Farley one of the greatest prognosticators the country had ever seen. Think of it, Mr. President, here in the United States the Postmaster General has said, "We will let the Senate talk." Certainly, our constituents ought to feel very grateful to the Postmaster General for permitting the Members of the Senate of the United States, whom they have elected to office, to speak their minds in the Senate. The constituents of the Members of the House of Representatives ought to feel very grateful to the Postmaster General for condescending to let their Representatives speak with reference to the bill.

Then men were sent into nearly every State in the Union to arouse the labor leaders for the purpose of having them send protests and denunciations of Members of the Senate of the United States who were opposed to the bill. Men were sent into my State. One man was sent there who went to every labor organization in the State. I am told that he was on the Government pay roll. He was seeking to persuade the labor organizations to adopt resolutions not only in favor of the President's bill, but denouncing me. They went even further than that; one of the farm leaders told me that for the first time in his life he was invited to the White House, and it was suggested to him that he should go out and line up the farm organizations in the Northwest against every Member of the House and every Member of the Senate who dared to voice his opposition to the President's bill.

Something has been said about propaganda. We found the Secretary of Agriculture, by the medium of the radio trying to line up the farmers of the country. Why? Not because he knew anything about the Court proposal, not because he was particularly interested in this piece of proposed legislation, but because the Congress of the United States had appropriated money and placed it in his hands to take care of the drought-stricken farmers or those in need of relief; he alone could disburse this money to them, and

the implication, of course, was that unless this bill should be passed then the farmers would not be able perhaps to get further appropriations from the Congress.

Then we find the Postmaster General lining up the postmasters throughout the country. We find Mr. Harry Hopkins, of the W.P.A., on the radio, talking about the Democratic Party and about the Court proposal. Why? Why should the head of Works Progress Administration of the United States be propagandizing and trying to influence the people on relief against Members of the Senate? Hopkins' great influence over relief clients comes from the fact that he disburses money to them. But who appropriated that money? Whose money was it? It was the money of the people of the United States, appropriated by the Congress and turned over to Mr. Hopkins, and yet he is stirring up W.P.A. workers and their dependents against Members of the Senate and Members of the House, and that is the only reason why Hopkins spoke.

That spirit of intolerance with reference to the pending bill has prevailed and pervaded the discussion right down to the present moment. Everyone who does not agree with the administration on this proposal or who disagrees with the Attorney General is denounced as an "economic royalist" and as one who has sold out to Wall Street.

Then we found the same spirit of intolerance prevailing in this Chamber yesterday, disclosed by the amazing situation which developed here. When the debate had been proceeding for only a couple of days and the opponents of the bill had not spoken at all, but had merely asked questions of the proponents of the bill who were talking, a practice which has been indulged in by the Senate from time immemorial, when no question of a filibuster was involved at all, but only bona-fide debate on the issues involved in the bill, we were confronted with a sudden appeal for strict application of the rules. Was it because the proponents of the bill are afraid of real debate?

Mr. Farley said, "We have the votes. It is in the bag." If it were "in the bag," why did the proponents desert it? It was deserted and the great prophet of the Democratic Party was wrong. They did not have the votes. They do not now have the votes. They do not want the original bill debated, because they know that upon legitimate debate they cannot sustain it. They know that while at the outset they undoubtedly had 60 votes in favor of the original bill, which would have added six new Justices to the Supreme Court, after the Members of the Senate heard or read the testimony of those appearing before the Judiciary Committee, and after they had studied the bill, one by one, and then two by two, and then by threes and fours, they deserted that bill, until on the day before yesterday the Democratic leader of the Senate announced that the reason why the proponents of the measure did not try to put forward the other bill was because they did not have the votes to pass it. They say they have enough votes at the present time to pass the compromise proposal, and then they appealed to party loyalty. They said to the new Senators who have just been elected, "You ought to vote for this bill because you rode in on the coattails of the President of the United States."

Thank God, I did not ride in on the coattails of the President of the United States! Thank God, I do not have to go to him and ask him whether or not I have to follow the Democratic leader in this new proposal! Those of you who rode in on the coattails of the President of the

United States will ride out on the coattails of the President of the United States if that is the only reason you are here.

I did not ride in on the coattails of any President of the United States. I did not come here because I had promised to be 100 percent for the administration and to vote for everything the President wanted.

There are those who were elected to the United States Senate on a platform of "100 percent Roosevelt," but after assuming their seats in this body, when it was politically expedient, they unhesitatingly cast their votes against the administration. Now, however, some such Senators assert that they must vote for this bill because of their campaign promise of supporting the President 100 percent — that pledge is one that they keep or follow, utilize or discard as they deem is politically expedient.

No, Mr. President, I did not come to the Senate on the coattails of anyone; I came to the Senate on my own, and I am responsible for what I do in the Senate. I expect the people of my State to hold me responsible for my actions; and if I go out, I will go out riding on my own coattails and not upon the coattails of anyone else.

Finally, Mr. President, we were told, "If you do not vote for this bill, you will break the President's heart." Oh, dear! What a pity! "You are going to break the President's heart if you do not vote for him on this bill."

If Senators are going to break the President's heart because they do not vote for him on this bill, they ought to go back and vote for six new judges instead of voting for the substitute, because we are told that this is not the President's bill. Oh, no; this is not his bill. This is not what the President wanted. He wanted six new judges. And why did he want six new judges? Because some of the proponents of the original bill said, "We cannot trust less than four judges, and we ought to have six because some of the six might go back on us; but if we cannot get six, the least we will take is four." Finally, however, they have come down and have said, "We do not want six all at one time. That was wrong. That was packing the Court; so now, instead of packing it all at once, we will pack it by slow motion, and we will get the same result."

There is not the slightest difference in principle between this bill and the other bill so far as the objectives sought to be attained by the proponents of the bills are concerned. The only distinction between the original and this substitute Court bill is that the latter packs the Supreme Court by slow motion. . . .

Incidentally, who was it that declared the second Frazier-Lemke Act unconstitutional? Whom do you suppose it was? Some judge appointed by this administration out in Illinois or Pennsylvania — appointed at the behest of the Senator from Pennsylvania or the Senator from Illinois, one or both of them — declared the law unconstitutional. The case went to the Supreme Court of the United States, and that Court declared the act constitutional.

After all, speaking of 5-to-4 decisions, do we want a Supreme Court that simply will agree entirely with our viewpoint? Is that what we want? Let me call attention to the fact that it is out of the clash of opinions that the truth comes. The worst thing that could happen to Congress, the worst thing that could happen to the country, would be to have but one strong political party. We get better legislation in this body because we have a clash of opinions as to proposed legislation. We get better bills out of commit-

tees when we have a clash of opinions. The American form of government depends upon the clash of opinions of its people, and not upon a subservient people who are voting as they are told to vote because they are getting handouts from the Treasury of the United States.

We are told that all the farmers of the country are for this measure. Let me say that I was out in Montana not long ago. Many farmers came to see me and said, "I am with the President. I do not know anything about this bill, but I am for it because I think the President wants it." Labor leaders came to me and said to me, "I am for the bill because I think the President wants it. I do not know anything about it." W.P.A. workers came to me and said, "I am on the public pay roll, and I want the bill because the President wants it. That is the reason." I say to the Members of the Senate, however, that practically every man with whom I have come in contact, from one end of the country to the other, who has given the question any serious thought or who knows anything about our problems or our Constitution is opposed to this measure.

If the contention of those who favor the bill is correct, why have a written Constitution at all? A great many persons in this country think there is not any need for a written Constitution; but why do we have one? We have one, my friends, because my forefathers, like the forefathers of most of the Senators, had left foreign shores, where they had seen the tyranny of one-man government in Europe. Some of them had been driven out of England by James I, who said to them, "Unless you conform, I will harass you out of the country"; and he did harass them until they left that country. He drove them to Holland, and then they came to America and settled upon the shores of this great country of ours. They fought the American Revolution; they spilled their blood and many of them died, all up and down the Atlantic seaboard, in order that you and I, their posterity, might have a democratic form of government assured by a written Constitution.

When the framers of the Constitution met in the assembly in Philadelphia they did not write the Constitution simply to protect themselves, but they remembered some of the things that had occurred before. They remembered the six men of Dorset and the six farm laborers who had assembled for the purpose of petitioning for higher wages, and were banished from England for so doing. So they wrote into the Constitution of the United States a provision that the right of free assemblage should be guaranteed in the United States of America.

They wrote it into the Constitution because those six men were banished from England and sent to Australia. They also wrote into the Constitution that no man should be banished from this country on account of crime. Remembering that Mary, Queen of Scots, before she was beheaded, asked and pleaded that she should be confronted with her accusers, they wrote into the Constitution of the United States that every accused person should be confronted by his accusers, that he should have the right of trial by jury, and that he should have the right to a writ of habeas corpus. They remembered that in European countries the army had been able to enter a man's home and take possession of it; so they wrote into the Constitution of the United States a provision to the effect that no general, no Army officer, no matter whom

he might be, in peacetime should be permitted to quarter his troops in the home of a citizen; and if he tried to do so, the citizen could say to him, "Go on down the road."

I might go on and enumerate the other provisions of the Bill of Rights, and say that because of what had been done in Europe the forefathers not only wanted to lay down those principles but they wanted to make those rights inalienable to the people of this country for all time to come.

Oh, but it is said, "What has that to do with the Court-packing bill?" If four men can be put upon the Supreme Bench to override the Constitution of the United States in one particular, they can say as to every other provision of the Constitution of the United States that it shall be inoperative. They can say whatever they choose to say, and make the Bill of Rights become as nothing to the people of this country. . . .

SENATOR JOSEPH C. O'MAHONEY

Mr. President, I was remarking that the pending measure in the nature of a substitute has been presented to this body without an explanation. I think it ought to be made clear to the Senate and to the country that we are not discussing a personal issue; we are discussing a system for the reorganization of the judiciary of the United States. The issue before this body is not the election of 1940, as some Senators seem to imagine; the issue before this body is not the New Deal, as some Senators would like to have the country believe; the issue before this body is not the record of Franklin D. Roosevelt, as some Senators would like us to believe. The issue before this body is whether or not we are going to adopt a system for the judiciary of the United

States vastly different from anything
which has ever existed in the history of
our Government.

We are rapidly approaching the one
hundred and fiftieth anniversary of the
adoption of the Constitution of the
United States under which our judicial
system was established; and we are now
asked to consider a bill which, if enacted,
would revolutionize that system. The
measure before us today and which will
be before us tomorrow and many a day
hence, I gather from the attitude of Senators, should not be entitled "A bill to
reform the judiciary," as it is sometimes
called in the public press; it should be
called a bill to centralize the administration of justice and to give the central
establishment at Washington greater
control over the local administration of
justice than it has ever had in this
democracy.

Do we desire to centralize the administration of justice? Presidents come and
Presidents go. The present occupant of
the White House will not always occupy
that distinguished position with the great
ability and charm with which he now
occupies it. Some other President will
succeed him, and when he does, if this
bill should become a law, it would apply
to him as well as to the present occupant
of the White House.

So I say, Mr. President, this is not a
personal issue; this is not a question of
whether or not we are going to give a
certain amount of power to Franklin D.
Roosevelt. The issue before us is whether
we are going to give this power to any
President who may occupy the White
House, no matter who he may be.

I shall not engage in any invidious
comparisons; I shall not mention names;
but there must come to the mind of every
Member of this body, as there must come

to the minds of all the citizens of the
United States, the names of Presidents in
whom they would not for 3 minutes en-
trust the power which is proposed to be
vested in the President by the pending
measure.

A New System Is Proposed

Remember we are acting upon a system. Let no one forget it. If this measure should be enacted into law, this
generation may pass and the next generation will be operating under the system
proposed, which would mark a revolutionary change from the system which
has been handed down to us by the constitutional fathers.

Let us consider the bill. What pro-
ponent has yet stood upon this floor and
explained the first section of the proposed
substitute? Was it explained by the sponsors of the bill? Did the eminent chairman of the Judiciary Committee of the
Senate of the United States, the Senator
from Arizona (Mr. Ashurst), whose name
is attached to this measure, explain the
bill? Did the eminent Senator from Kentucky (Mr. Logan), whose name is
attached to this measure, rise in his place
to explain its purport and effect? He
spoke not a single word of that character.
Did the Senator from New Mexico (Mr.
Hatch), who lends his name to it, give
any explanation of the measure? Not a
word or a syllable. And when those of us
who are opposed to the measure undertake to discuss it we are told that we are
filibusterers and are preventing the transaction of the public business.

What business can be more important,
Senators of the United States, than the
establishment of the judicial system under which you, your children, and your
children's children will be governed so
long as this measure remains upon the

statute books, if it is passed? Good Presidents come and good Presidents go, and bad Presidents come and bad Presidents go, and the power that is proposed to be vested by this bill in any occupant of the White House could be used by a man, if he were so minded, to wreck every vestige of human liberty under the Stars and Stripes. Let us consider it.

When the original bill was proposed it provided that in the instance of each member of the judiciary who had attained the age of 70 years and had served for 10 years and within 6 months had not retired or resigned, the President should appoint another Justice.

It was mandatory. He had no discretion about it at all. The solemn duty was laid upon him by the terms of the bill to send the nomination to the Senate of the United States for every man on the bench of the given age and service. As it was written it would probably have resulted in the immediate appointment of six Justices.

Discretionary Appointments

The resentment of the country to the plan was so sweeping and so strong that it was abandoned, or at least we are told it was abandoned, and here as a substitute we have a bill which, instead of saying that the President "shall" appoint, says he "may" appoint. The President now has the discretion to appoint an additional Justice when a sitting Justice reaches the age of 75 years. Why the discretion? Is the President to be permitted to say, "In my judgment new blood is not necessary now. It is true these men are 75 years of age. It is true that there ought to be new blood; but I am satisfied. I shall make no appointments."

Understand, Mr. President, I am speaking in an impersonal manner. I am not speaking of the present occupant of the White House. I am speaking of any occupant of the White House. If the power is discretionary then it follows as the night follows the day that the occupant of the White House at some future time, if not at this time, may say, "I am satisfied with the decisions of Justice A, who is 75 years of age, and I shall not send a new nomination."

Why the difference between "shall" and "may"? When it was pointed out on the first day of the debate, the Senator from New Mexico (Mr. Hatch) immediately announced his belief that the appointment should be mandatory, and I understand now from the newspapers that the Senator from Kentucky (Mr. Logan) says the same thing. How does it happen that, after the lapse of all these months, the proponents of the substitute come upon the floor not knowing exactly what the bill proposes? Who is the legislative draftsman who substituted "may" for "shall"? It was not the chairman of the Judiciary Committee (Mr. Ashurst). It was not the Senator from New Mexico (Mr. Hatch). It was not the Senator from Kentucky (Mr. Logan). It was not the Senator from Arkansas (Mr. Robinson) who proposed the substitute. Who substituted "may" for "shall"?

The Accumulation of Appointments

That is not all. The new bill provides that:

Not more than one appointment of an additional Justice as herein authorized shall be made in any calendar year.

What is the explanation for that limitation? Obviously if new blood is necessary, if age be a crime, if, when Justices reach the age of 75 they are no longer fit to sit upon the bench, why should they not be removed and why should there be only one substitute Justice when perhaps there may be four or five who have reached the alleged age of senility? If the rule is good for one it is good for all.

Oh, but this limitation was put in for the purpose of preventing judgments of the Court from being influenced by the appointments. How simple-minded we are all supposed to be! . . .

Mr. President, we have here a substitute which provides, first, for concentration of power by giving the appointing authority wholly new powers in the selection of Justices of the Supreme Court in the manner I have described; for concentration of power in the transfer of judges, both circuit and district, through all parts of the country; for additional concentration of power through the operation of the newly established office of proctor; and, finally — the fourth phase of concentration — permission to the United States Government to intervene in every case in which the constitutionality of a law is drawn in question, and to appeal these cases, regardless of the desires or will of the litigants.

Does this consolidation have any significance for the people of the United States? I think it cannot be denied that it does. It has a tremendous significance, a significance which I venture to say is not realized by many persons in the United States. Perhaps not many in Congress or in the administration realize the great danger that confronts them. . . .

There is no Member of this body who does not know that the great glory of the American judicial system is the independence of the courts. The independent judiciary was the greatest advance in the history of government, and it has been one of our great prides that it has been protected in the United States, and that it is the ideal of our people.

Independent Judiciary Essential

Mr. President, I suppose there is no great statesman of our country who has not at one time or another declared his belief in the independence of the courts. In the same month in which the Declaration of Independence was signed, Thomas Jefferson wrote a letter to the distinguished George Wythe, of Virginia, from which I wish to read an extract. It was dated July 1776 and reads:

The dignity and stability of government in all its branches, the morals of the people, and every blessing of society, depends so much upon an upright and skillful administration of justice that the judicial power ought to be distinct from both the legislature and executive, and independent upon both, that so it may be a check upon both, as both should be checks upon that. The judges, therefore, should always be men of learning and experience in the laws, of exemplary morals, great patience, calmness, and attention; their minds should not be distracted with jarring interests: they should not be dependent upon any man or body of men. To these ends they should hold estates for life in their offices, or, in other words, their commissions should be during good behavior, and their salaries ascertained and established by law.

For misbehavior, the grand inquest of the colony, the house of representatives, should impeach them before the Governor and council, when they should have time and opportunity to make their defense; but if convicted, should be removed from their offices and subjected to such other punishment as shall be thought proper.

Every law student who remembers his Blackstone remembers the lectures of that distinguished British jurist and his pronouncement upon this subject. I quote from Blackstone's Commentaries, volume 1, chapter 7, page 268:

In this distinct and separate existence of the judicial power in a peculiar body of men, nominated indeed, but not removable at pleasure, by the crown, consists one main preservative of the public liberty; which cannot subsist long in any state unless the administration of common justice be in some degree separated from the legislative and also from the executive power. Were it joined with the legislative, the life, liberty, and property of the subject would be in the hands of arbitrary judges, whose decisions would be then regulated only by their own opinions, and not by any fundamental principles of law; which, though legislators may depart from, yet judges are bound to observe. Were it joined with the executive, this union might soon be an overbalance for the legislative. For which reason, by the statute of 16 Car. I., c. 10, which abolished the court of star chamber, effectual care is taken to remove all judicial power out of the hands of the King's privy council, who, as then was evident from recent instances, might soon be inclined to pronounce that for law which was most agreeable to the prince or his officers.

Nothing, therefore, is more to be avoided, in a free constitution, than uniting the provinces of a judge and a minister of state. . . .

The object of the creation of the independent judiciary — and I could quote at length from the distinguished statesmen of the past — was to preserve the individual citizen from the power of the Government. That is the purpose of the independent judiciary, to make the judges free of the executive arm so that there may be no danger of a miscarriage, so that there may be no danger that the executive arm of the Government may impose its will in decision of cases. But now we have a bill before us which tears this principle down and tends to make the judiciary the agent of the Government. Do you wonder I call it revolutionary?

THE SUPREME COURT MAJORITY
CHANGES ITS MIND

A. ADKINS *v.* CHILDREN'S HOSPITAL
Mr. Justice Sutherland delivered the opinion of the court [majority opinion]:

THE question presented for determination by these appeals is the constitutionality of the Act of September 19, 1918, providing for the fixing of minimum wages for women and children in the District of Columbia. . . .

The judicial duty of passing upon the constitutionality of an act of Congress is one of great gravity and delicacy. The statute here in question has successfully

261 U. S. 525, 43 Sup. Rep. 394.

borne the scrutiny of the legislative branch of the government, which, by enacting it, has affirmed its validity; and that determination must be given great weight. This court, by an unbroken line of decisions from Chief Justice Marshall to the present day, has steadily adhered to the rule that every possible presumption is in favor of the validity of an act of Congress until overcome beyond rational doubt. But if, by clear and indubitable demonstration, a statute be opposed to the Constitution, we have no choice but to say so. The Constitution, by its own terms, is the supreme law of the land, emanating from the people, the repository of ultimate sovereignty under our form of government. A congressional statute, on the other hand, is the act of an agency of this sovereign authority, and, if it conflict with the Constitution, must fall; for that which is not supreme must yield to that which is. To hold it invalid (if it be invalid) is a plain exercise of the judicial power, — that power vested in courts to enable them to administer justice according to law. . . .

The statute now under consideration is attacked upon the ground that it authorizes an unconstitutional interference with the freedom of contract included within the guaranties of the due process clause of the 5th Amendment. That the right to contract about one's affairs is a part of the liberty of the individual protected by this clause is settled by the decisions of this court, and is no longer open to question. . . . Within this liberty are contracts of employment of labor. In making such contracts, generally speaking, the parties have an equal right to obtain from each other the best terms they can as the result of private bargaining. . . .

There is, of course, no such thing as absolute freedom of contract. It is subject to a great variety of restraints. But freedom of contract is, nevertheless, the general rule and restraint the exception; and the exercise of legislative authority to abridge it can be justified only by the existence of exceptional circumstances. . . .

The essential characteristics of the statute now under consideration, which differentiate it from the laws fixing hours of labor, will be made to appear as we proceed. . . . A law forbidding work to continue beyond a given number of hours leaves the parties free to contract about wages and thereby equalize whatever additional burdens may be imposed upon the employer as a result of the restrictions as to hours, by an adjustment in respect of the amount of wages. Enough has been said to show that the authority to fix hours of labor cannot be exercised except in respect of those occupations where work of long-continued duration is detrimental to health. This court has been careful in every case where the question has been raised, to place its decision upon this limited authority of the legislature to regulate hours of labor, and to disclaim any purpose to uphold the legislation as fixing wages, thus recognizing an essential difference between the two. It seems plain that these decisions afford no real support for any form of law establishing minimum wages.

If now, in the light furnished by the foregoing exceptions to the general rule forbidding legislative interference with freedom of contract, we examine and analyze the statute in question, we shall see that it differs from them in every material respect. It is not a law dealing with any business charged with a public interest or with public work, or to meet and tide over a temporary emergency. It has nothing to do with the character, methods, or periods of wage payments. It does not prescribe hours of labor or conditions under which labor is to be done. It is not for the protection of persons under legal disability, or for the prevention of fraud. It is simply and exclusively a price-fixing law, confined to adult women (for we are not now considering the provisions relating to minors), who are legally as capable of contracting for themselves as men. It forbids two parties having lawful capacity — under penalties as to the employer — to freely contract with one another in respect of the price for which one shall render service to the other in a purely private employment where both are willing, perhaps anxious, to agree, even though the consequences may be to oblige one to surrender a desirable engagement, and the other to dispense with the services of a desirable employee. The price fixed by the board need have no relation to the capacity or earning power of the employee, the number of hours which may happen to constitute the day's work, the character of the place where the work is to be done, or the circumstances or surroundings of the employment; and, while it has no other basis to support its validity than the assumed necessities of the employee, it takes no account of any independent resources she may have. It is based wholly on the opinions of the members of the board and their advisers — perhaps an average of their opinions, if they do not precisely agree — as to what will be necessary to provide a living for a woman, keep her in health, and preserve her morals. It applies to any and every occupation in the District, without regard to its nature or the character of the work.

The standard furnished by the statute for the guidance of the board is so vague as to be impossible of practical application with any reasonable degree of accuracy. What is sufficient to supply the necessary cost of living for a woman worker and maintain her in good health and protect her morals is obviously not a precise or unvarying sum, not even approximately so. The amount will depend upon a variety of circumstances: The individual temperament, habits of thrift, care, ability to buy necessaries intelligently, and whether the woman live alone or with her family. To those who practise economy, a given sum will afford comfort, while to those of contrary habit the same sum will be wholly inadequate. The cooperative economies of the family group are not taken into account, though they constitute an important consideration in estimating the cost of living, for it is obvious that the individual expense will be less in the case of a member of a family than in the case of one living alone. The relation between earnings and morals is not capable of standardization. It cannot be shown that well-paid women safeguard their morals more carefully than those who are poorly paid. Morality rests upon other considerations than wages; and there is, certainly, no such prevalent connection between the two as to justify a broad attempt to adjust the latter with reference to the former. As a means of safeguarding the morals the attempted classification, in our opinion, is without reasonable basis. No distinction can be made between women who work for others and those who do not; nor is there ground for distinction between women and men; for, certainly, if women require a minimum wage to preserve their morals, men require it to preserve their honesty. For these reasons, and others which might be stated, the inquiry in respect of the necessary cost of living and of the income necessary to preserve health and morals presents an individual, and not a composite, question, and must be answered for each individual, considered by herself, and not by a general formula prescribed by a statutory bureau.

This uncertainty of the statutory standard is demonstrated by a consideration of certain orders of the board already made. These orders fix the sum to be paid to a woman employed in a place where food is served or in a mercantile establishment, at $16.50 per week; in a printing establishment, at $15.50 per week; and in a laundry, at $15 per week, with a provision reducing this to $9 in the case of a beginner. If a woman employed to serve food requires a minimum of $16.50 per week, it is hard to understand how the same woman working in a printing establishment or in a laundry is to get on with an income lessened by from $1 to $7.50 per week. The board probably found it impossible to follow the indefinite standard of the statute, and brought other and different factors into the problem; and this goes far in the direction of demonstrating the fatal uncertainty of the act, — an infirmity which, in our opinion, plainly exists.

The law takes account of the necessities of only one party to the contract. It ignores the necessities of the employer by compelling him to pay not less than a certain sum, not only whether the employee is capable of earning it, but irrespective of the ability of his business to sustain the burden, generously leaving him, of course, the privilege of abandoning his business as an alternative for going on at a loss. Within the limits of the minimum sum, he is precluded, under penalty of the fine and imprisonment, from adjusting compensation to the differing merits of his employees. It compels him to pay at least the sum fixed in any event, because the employee needs it, but requires no service of equivalent value from the employee. It therefore undertakes to solve but one half of the problem. The other half is the establishment of a corresponding standard of efficiency; and this forms no part of the policy of the legislation, although in practice the former half without the latter must lead to ultimate failure, in accordance with the inexorable law that no one can continue indefinitely to take out more

than he puts in without ultimately exhausting the supply. The law is not confined to the great and powerful employers, but embraces those whose bargaining power may be as weak as that of the employee. It takes no account of periods of stress and business depression, of crippling losses, which may leave the employer himself without adequate means of livelihood. To the extent that the sum fixed exceeds the fair value of the services rendered, it amounts to a compulsory exaction from the employer for the support of a partially indigent person, for whose condition there rests upon him no peculiar responsibility, and therefore, in effect, arbitrarily shifts to his shoulders a burden which, if it belongs to anybody, belongs to society as a whole.

The feature of this statute which, perhaps more than any other, puts upon it the stamp of invalidity is that it exacts from the employer an arbitrary payment for a purpose and upon a basis having no causal connection with his business, or the contract, or the work the employee engages to do. The declared basis, as already pointed out, is not the value of the service rendered, but the extraneous circumstance that the employee needs to get a prescribed sum of money to insure her subsistence, health, and morals. The ethical right of every worker, man or woman, to a living wage, may be conceded. One of the declared and important purposes of trade organizations is to secure it. And with that principle and with every legitimate effort to realize it in fact, no one can quarrel; but the fallacy of the proposed method of attaining it is that it assumes that every employer is bound, at all events, to furnish it. The moral requirement, implicit in every contract of employment, viz., that the amount to be paid and the service to be rendered shall bear to each other some relation of just equivalence, is completely ignored. The necessities of the employee are alone considered, and these arise outside of the employment, are the same when there is no employment, and as great in one occupation as in another. Certainly the employer, by paying a fair equivalent for the service rendered, though not sufficient to support the employee, has neither caused nor contributed to her poverty. On the contrary, to the extent of what he pays, he has relieved it. In principle, there can be no difference between the case of selling labor and the case of selling goods. If one goes to the butcher, the baker, or grocer to buy food, he is morally entitled to obtain the worth of his money, but he is not entitled to more. If what he gets is worth what he pays, he is not justified in demanding more simply because he needs more; and the shopkeeper, having dealt fairly and honestly in that transaction, is not concerned in any peculiar sense with the question of his customer's necessities. Should a statute undertake to vest in a commission power to determine the quantity of food necessary for individual support, and require the shopkeeper, if he sell to the individual at all, to furnish that quantity at not more than a fixed maximum, it would undoubtedly fall before the constitutional test. The fallacy of any argument in support of the validity of such a statute would be quickly exposed. The argument in support of that now being considered is equally fallacious, though the weakness of it may not be so plain. A statute requiring an employer to pay in money, to pay at prescribed and regular intervals, to pay the value of the services rendered, even to pay with fair relation to the extent of the benefit obtained from the service, would be understandable. But a statute which prescribes payment with-

out regard to any of these things, and solely with relation to circumstances apart from the contract of employment, the business affected by it, and the work done under it, is so clearly the product of a naked, arbitrary exercise of power, that it cannot be allowed to stand under the Constitution of the United States. . . .

It is said that great benefits have resulted from the operation of such statutes, not alone in the District of Columbia, but in the several states where they have been in force. A mass of reports, opinions of special observers and students of the subject, and the like, has been brought before us in support of this statement, all of which we have found interesting but only mildly persuasive. That the earnings of women now are greater than they were formerly, and that conditions affecting women have become better in other respects, may be conceded; but convincing indications of the logical relation of these desirable changes to the law in question are significantly lacking. They may be, and quite probably are, due to other causes. We cannot close our eyes to the notorious fact that earnings everywhere, in all occupations, have greatly increased, — not alone in states where the minimum wage law obtains, but in the country generally, — quite as much or more among men as among women, and in occupations outside the reach of the law as in those governed by it. No real test of the economic value of the law can be had during periods of maximum employment, when general causes keep wages up to or above the minimum; that will come in periods of depression and struggle for employment, when the efficient will be employed at the minimum rate, while the less capable may not be employed at all.

Finally, it may be said that if, in the interest of the public welfare, the police power may be invoked to justify the fixing of a minimum wage, it may, when the public welfare is thought to require it, be invoked to justify a maximum wage. The power to fix high wages connotes, by like course of reasoning, the power to fix low wages. If, in the face of the guaranties of the 5th Amendment, this form of legislation shall be legally justified, the field for the operation of the police power will have been widened to a great and dangerous degree. If, for example, in the opinion of future lawmakers, wages in the building trades shall become so high as to preclude people of ordinary means from building and owning homes, an authority which sustains the minimum wage will be invoked to support a maximum wage for building laborers and artisans, and the same argument which has been here urged to strip the employer of his constitutional liberty of contract in one direction will be utilized to strip the employee of his constitutional liberty of contract in the opposite direction. A wrong decision does not end with itself: it is a precedent, and, with the swing of sentiment, its bad influence may run from one extremity of the arc to the other.

It has been said that legislation of the kind now under review is required in the interest of social justice, for whose ends freedom of contract may lawfully be subjected to restraint. The liberty of the individual to do as he pleases, even in innocent matters, is not absolute. It must frequently yield to the common good, and the line beyond which the power of interference may not be pressed is neither definite nor unalterable, but may be made to move, within limits not well defined, with changing need and circumstance. Any attempt to fix a rigid boundary would be unwise as well as futile. But, nevertheless, there are limits to the power, and when these have been passed, it becomes the plain duty of the courts, in the proper exercise of their authority, to so declare. To sustain the individual freedom of action contemplated by the Constitution is not to strike down the common good, but to exalt it; for surely the good of society as a whole cannot be better served than by the preservation against arbitrary restraint of the liberties of its constituent members.

It follows from what has been said that the act in question passes the limit prescribed by the Constitution, and, accordingly, the decrees of the court below are affirmed. . . .

B. WEST COAST HOTEL COMPANY v. PARRISH
Mr. Chief Justice Hughes delivered the opinion of the court [majority opinion]:

This case presents the question of the constitutional validity of the minimum wage law of the State of Washington. . . .

The principle which must control our decision is not in doubt. The constitutional provision invoked is the due process clause of the Fourteenth Amendment governing the States, as the due process clause invoked in the Adkins Case gov-

300 U. S. 379, 57 S. Ct. 578.

erned Congress. In each case the violation alleged by those attacking minimum wage regulation for women is deprivation of freedom of contract. What is this freedom? The Constitution does not speak of freedom of contract. It speaks of liberty and prohibits the deprivation of liberty without due process of law. In prohibiting that deprivation the Constitution does not recognize an absolute and uncontrollable liberty. Liberty in each of its phases has its history and connotation. But the liberty safeguarded is liberty in a social organization which requires the protection of law against the evils which menace the health, safety, morals and welfare of the people. Liberty under the Constitution is thus necessarily subject to the restraints of due process, and regulation which is reasonable in relation to its subject and is adopted in the interests of the community is due process.

This essential limitation of liberty in general governs freedom of contract in particular. More than twenty-five years ago we set forth the applicable principle in these words, after referring to the cases where the liberty guaranteed by the Fourteenth Amendment had been broadly described:

But it was recognized in the cases cited, as in many others, that freedom of contract is a qualified and not an absolute right. There is no absolute freedom to do as one wills or to contract as one chooses. The guaranty of liberty does not withdraw from legislative supervision that wide department of activity which consists of the making of contracts, or deny to government the power to provide restrictive safeguards. Liberty implies the absence of arbitrary restraint, not immunity from reasonable regulations and prohibitions imposed in the interests of the community. . . .

It is manifest that this established principle is peculiarly applicable in relation to the employment of women in whose protection the State has a special interest. That phase of the subject received elaborate consideration in Muller v. Oregon, . . . where the constitutional authority of the State to limit the working hours of women was sustained. We emphasized the consideration that "woman's physical structure and the performance of maternal functions place her at a disadvantage in the struggle for subsistence" and that her physical well-being "becomes an object of public interest and care in order to preserve the strength and vigor of the race." We emphasized the need of protecting woman against oppression despite her possession of contractual rights. We said that "though limitations upon personal and contractual rights may be removed by legislation, there is that in her disposition and habits of life which will operate against a full assertion of those rights. She will still be where some legislation to protect her seems necessary to secure a real equality of right." Hence she was "properly placed in a class by herself, and legislation designed for her protection may be sustained even when like legislation is not necessary for men and could not be sustained." We concluded that the limitations which the statute there in question "placed upon her contractual powers, upon her right to agree with her employer as to the time she shall labor" were "not imposed solely for her benefit, but also largely for the benefit of all." Again, in Quong Wing v. Kirkendall, . . . in referring to a differentiation with respect to the employment of women, we said that the Fourteenth Amendment did not interfere with state power by creating a "fictitious equality." We referred to recognized classifications on the basis of sex with regard to hours of work and in other matters, and we observed that the particular points at which that difference shall be enforced by legislation were largely in the power of the State. In later rulings this Court sustained the regulation of hours of work of women employees in Riley v. Massachusetts, . . . (factories); Miller v. Wilson, . . . (hotels); and Bosley v. McLaughlin . . . (hospitals).

This array of precedents and the principles they applied were thought by the dissenting Justices in the Adkins Case to demand that the minimum wage statute be sustained. The validity of the distinction made by the Court between a minimum wage and a maximum of hours in limiting liberty of contract was especially challenged. . . . That challenge persists and is without any satisfactory answer. As Chief Justice Taft observed: "In absolute freedom of contract the one term is as important as the other, for both enter equally into the consideration given and received; a restriction as to one is not any greater in essence than the other, and is of the same kind. One is the multiplier and the other the multiplicand." And Mr. Justice Holmes, while recognizing that "the distinctions of the law are distinctions of degree," could "perceive no difference in the kind or degree of interference with liberty, the only matter with which we have any concern, between the one case and the other. The bargain is equally affected whichever half you regulate.". . .

The minimum wage to be paid under the Washington statute is fixed after full consideration by representatives of employers, employees and the public. It may be assumed that the minimum wage is fixed in consideration of the services that are performed in the particular occupations under normal conditions. Provision is made for special licenses at less wages in the case of women who are incapable of full service. The statement of Mr. Justice Holmes in the Adkins Case is pertinent: "This statute does not compel anybody to pay anything. It simply forbids employment at rates below those fixed as the minimum requirement of health and right living. It is safe to assume that women will not be employed at even the lowest wages allowed unless they earn them, or unless the employer's business can sustain the burden. In short the law in its character and operation is like hundreds of so-called police laws that have been upheld. . . ." And Chief Justice Taft forcibly pointed out the consideration which is basic in a statute of this character: "Legislatures which adopt a requirement of maximum hours or minimum wages may be presumed to believe that when sweating employers are prevented from paying unduly low wages by positive law they will continue their business, abating that part of their profits, which were wrung from the necessities of their employees, and will concede the better terms required by the law; and that while in individual cases hardship may result, the restriction will enure to the benefit of the general class of employees in whose interest the law is passed and so to that of the community at large. . . ."

With full recognition of the earnestness and vigor which characterize the prevailing opinion in the Adkins Case, we find it impossible to reconcile that ruling with these well-considered declarations. What can be closer to the public interest than the health of women and their protection from unscrupulous and overreaching employers? And if the protection of women is a legitimate end of the exercise of state power, how can it be said that the requirement of the payment of a minimum wage fairly fixed in order to meet the very necessities of existence is not an admissible means to that end? The legislature of the State was clearly entitled to consider the situation of women in employment, the fact that they are in the class receiving the least pay, that their bargaining power is relatively weak, and that they are ready victims of those who would take advantage of their necessitous circumstances. The legislature was entitled to adopt measures to reduce the evils of the "sweating system," the exploiting of workers at wages so low as to be insufficient to meet the bare cost of living, thus making their very helplessness the occasion of a most injurious competition. The legislature had the right to consider that its minimum wage requirements would be an important aid in carrying out its policy of protection. The adoption of similar requirements by many States evidences a deep-seated conviction both as to the presence of the evil and as to the means adopted to check it. Legislative response to that conviction cannot be regarded as arbitrary or capricious and that is all we have to decide. Even if the wisdom of the policy be regarded as debatable and its effects uncertain, still the legislature is entitled to its judgment.

There is an additional and compelling consideration which recent economic experience has brought into a strong light. The exploitation of a class of workers who are in an unequal position with respect to bargaining power and are thus relatively defenceless against the denial of a living wage is not only detrimental to their health and well-being but casts a direct burden for their support upon the community. What these workers lose in wages the taxpayers are called upon to pay. The bare cost of living must be met. We may take judicial notice of the unparalleled demands for relief which arose during the recent period of depression and still continue to an alarming extent despite the degree of economic recovery which has been achieved. It is unnecessary to cite official statistics to establish what is of common knowledge through the length and breadth of the land. While in the instant case no factual brief has been presented, there is no reason to doubt that the State of Washington has encountered the same social problem that is present elsewhere. The community is not bound to provide what is in effect a subsidy for unconscionable employers. The community may direct its law-making power to correct the abuse which springs from their selfish disregard of the public interest. The argument that the legislation in question constitutes an arbitrary discrimination, because it does not extend to men, is unavailing. This Court has frequently held that the legislative authority, acting within its proper field, is not bound to extend its regulation to all cases which it might possibly reach. The legislature "is free to recognize degrees of harm and it may confine its restrictions to those classes of cases where the need is deemed to be clearest." If "the law presumably hits the evil where it is most felt, it is not to be overthrown because there are other instances to which it might have been applied." There is no "doctrinaire requirement" that the legislation should be couched in all embracing terms. . . .

Our conclusion is that the case of Adkins v. Children's Hospital, supra, . . . should be, and it is, overruled. The judgment of the Supreme Court of the State of Washington is affirmed. . . .

Suggestions for Additional Reading

Aside from materials from which selections are presented here there are other books which deal historically with the Supreme Court with particular purposes in mind. Among these are: Dean Alfange, *The Supreme Court and the National Will* (Garden City, 1937), which deals with the question of whether or not the Court, in the long run, truly represents the "will of the people"; and H. B. Levy, *Our Constitution: Tool or Testament* (New York, 1941), where an attempt is made to discover what effects, if any, a judge's personal philosophy has on his judicial decision. A shorter book of interest, which gives the viewpoint of one of the leading judges on the Bench is Charles Evans Hughes, *The Supreme Court of the United States* (New York, 1936).

As in the historical field, there are many useful books to choose from which deal with the question of judicial review. Still outstanding in this field is the brilliant contribution of Charles Grove Haines, *The American Doctrine of Judicial Supremacy* (Berkeley, 1932). See, also, by the same author, *The Revival of Natural Law Concepts* (Cambridge, 1930), chapters 4–8. Along the same lines see Benjamin F. Wright, *American Interpretations of Natural Law* (Cambridge, 1931). One of the earliest books dealing with this question, written at the height of another national debate over the correct place of the Court in the American system of government, is Charles A. Beard, *The Supreme Court and the Constitution* (New York, 1912). Mr. Beard attempts

to prove that the system of judicial review, as we know it, was undoubtedly the intent of the framers of the Constitution. For an opposite point of view, see Louis B. Boudin, *Government by Judiciary* (New York, 1932). In this two-volume effort, we find many of the arguments against the Court later cited by the proponents of President Roosevelt's reorganization plan. Another outstanding work in this field is Robert K. Carr, *The Supreme Court and Judicial Review* (New York, 1942). This is especially worthwhile for those interested in the nature of the Court's power and what influences have shaped its decisions.

At the height of the nationwide furor over the President's bill, countless words were written on both sides of the issue. For an exceptionally clear picture of the entire Court struggle, it would be wise to consult three books written by Edward Samuel Corwin: *Court over Constitution* (Princeton, 1938), *The Twilight of the Supreme Court* (New Haven, 1937), *Constitutional Revolution, Ltd.* (Claremont, 1941). For an exceptionally vehement attack on the Court (and, at the same time, a strong defense of the President's position) see I. F. Stone, *The Court Disposes* (New York, 1937). For an equally passionate bit of writing representing the exactly opposite point of view, see Merlo J. Pusey, *The Supreme Court Crisis* (New York, 1937). Other books which attacked the "packing scheme" were: Walter Lippmann, *The Supreme Court: Independent or Controlled?* (New York, 1937), a collection of some of his newspaper columns; David Lawrence, *Supreme Court or Political Puppets?* New York, 1936); D. W. Johnson, *The Assault on the Supreme Court* (New York, 1937). Other books written at the time which have cogent sections dealing with the Court fight are: Morris L. Ernst, *The Ultimate Power* (Garden City, 1937), chapters 23–27; Ernest S. Bates, *The Story of the Supreme Court* (New York, 1936), preface and Chapter XI; William Y. Elliott, *The Need for Constitutional Reform* (New York, 1935), chapters 7–9; Irving Brant, *Storm over the Constitution* (New York, 1937). A few years after the tumult had subsided, there appeared a very interesting book by Robert H. Jackson, himself destined for the Bench at a later date, *The Struggle for Judicial Supremacy* (New York, 1941), which traces the growth of the Court as a political power and the growth of popular discontent with the Court culminating in the row of 1937. From the student's point of view, a challenging summary of this entire issue can be found in a book edited by William R. Barnes and A. W. Littlefield, *The Supreme Court Issue and the Constitution* (New York, 1937). In this small volume, the editors have succeeded in bringing together the following interesting items: quotations from numerous leading Americans stating their positions pro and con, historical statements on this issue whenever it has arisen in past American history, a short biography of all the men on the Court at the time of the debate, and charts dealing with former and contemporary Congressional and Court relationships. For those interested in the history of early attacks on the Supreme Court, see Charles Warren, "Legislative and Judicial Attacks on the Supreme Court," *American Law Review,* Vol. 47 (1913), pp. 1–34, 161–89. In the last few years, there have appeared a number of books on the era under discussion which deal with it in retrospect. These include C. Herman Pritchett, *The Roosevelt Court* (New York, 1948); Wesley McCune, *Nine Young Men* (New York, 1947), particularly chapters 1–5; C. Curtis, *Lions Under the Throne* (Boston, 1947), with emphasis on chapters 10–12; and Paul Freund, *On Understanding the Supreme Court* (Boston, 1950), part I only.

For those who would like to study the era by inspecting closely the lives of some of the men involved, any of the followings books are recommended: Samuel J. Konefsky, *Chief Justice Stone and the Supreme Court* (New York, 1949); Alpheus T. Mason, *Brandeis: A Free Man's Life* (New York, 1946); Cortez Ewing, *Judges of the Supreme Court* (Minneapolis, 1938).

For an analysis of, and excerpts from, the many decisions cited in this volume, see Robert E. Cushman, *Leading Constitutional Decisions* (New York, 1940).

A full bibliographical list may be obtained by consulting The United States Library of Congress, Division of Bibliography, for *The Supreme Court Issue* compiled by Florence S. Hellman (Washington, D. C., 1938).